Singing of Psalms a Gospel Ordinance
By John Cotton

Singing of Psalms a Gospel Ordinance
By John Cotton

Edited and updated by C. Matthew McMahon and Therese B. McMahon
Transcribed by Rylan Perkins

Copyright © 2013 by Puritan Publications and A Puritan's Mind

Some language and grammar has been updated from the original manuscript. Any change in wording or punctuation has not changed the intent or meaning of the original author(s), and has been made to aid the modern reader.

Published by Puritan Publications
A Ministry of A Puritan's Mind
4101 Coral Tree Circle #214
Coconut Creek, FL 33073
www.puritanshop.com
www.apuritansmind.com
www.puritanpublications.com

All rights reserved. No part of this publication may be reproduced, stored in a retrieval system or transmitted in any form by any means, electronic, mechanical, photocopy, recording or otherwise, without the prior permission of the publisher, except as provided by USA copyright law.

This Print Edition, 2013
Electronic Edition, 2013
Manufactured in the United States of America

ISBN: 978-1-937466-47-3
eISBN: 978-1-937466-46-6

TABLE OF CONTENTS

MEET JOHN COTTON 4

OF THE SINGING OF PSALMS CHAPTER 1: *Several Questions*.. 9

CHAPTER 2: *Propounding and clearing the second proof for singing Psalms with a lively voice.* 20

CHAPTER 3: *Propounding and clearing the third proof, for singing Psalms with a lively voice.* 24

CHAPTER 4: *Propounding the Second Question, stating and proving it.*.. 32

CHAPTER 5: *Clearing Objections* 36

CHAPTER 6: *Propounding a second and third argument, for the singing of David's Psalms.* 67

CHAPTER 7: *Concerning the singers. And first, whether one above to sing, or the whole Church.* 70

CHAPTER 8: *Whether women may sing as well as men.* 78

CHAPTER 9: *Whether carnal men may sing, as well as godly Christians?* 81

CHAPTER 10: *Of the manner of singing.* 98

CHAPTER 11: *Of reading the Psalms in order before Singing.*............ 111

CHAPTER 12: *Answering the Objections brought from the ancient practice of the Primitive Churches.* 115

MEET JOHN COTTON

John Cotton (1585-1662) was an English clergyman and colonist who left Puritan England for the "new world." He was a principal figure among the New England Pilgrim ministers, who also included Thomas Hooker, Increase Mather (who became his son-in-law), John Davenport, and Thomas Shepard and John Norton, who wrote his first biography. Cotton was the grandfather of Cotton Mather, who was named after him.

Born in England, he was educated at Derby School, in buildings which are now the Derby Heritage Centre, and attended Trinity College, Cambridge and Emmanuel College, Cambridge, where he became a Fellow in 1606. He became a long-serving minister in the English town of Boston, Lincolnshire before his Puritanism and criticism of hierarchy drew the hostile attention of the Church of England authorities. In 1633 William Laud was appointed Archbishop of Canterbury, and like numerous other Puritan nonconformist figures, Cotton soon came under his close "eye of scrutiny". In the same year Cotton, his family, and a few local followers sailed for the Massachusetts Bay Colony as pilgrims.

The Brownist congregational movement within the Church of England had by this stage, in effect at least, become a separate church. Because of his early views on the primacy of congregational government, his was an important role in Puritan aspirations to become an example to help reform the English church. He is best known among other things for his initial defense of Anne Hutchinson early in her trials during the Antinomian crisis, during which she mentioned him with respect, though he turned strongly against her with the further course of the trial. He is also remembered for his role in the banishment of Roger Williams regarding the role of democracy and the separation of church and state in the Puritan theonomic society, both of which Williams tended to advocate. Cotton grew still more conservative in his views with the years but always retained the estimation of his community.

Because of his popularity and previous Puritan leanings, he was invited to attend the Westminster Assembly of Divines. He was keen to go, though John Winthrop said that he could not see the point of "travelling 3,000 miles to agree with three men." The three men Winthrop refers to were the congregational representatives in the Assembly. Westminster was made up largely of Presbyterians. Cotton's desire to attend changed with the unfolding events of the First English Civil War, and he came to believe that he could be more effective in influencing the Assembly through his writings. He died in Boston, Massachusetts on December 23, 1652; the cause of death is unknown.

Some of the key works of John Cotton *are:*

1. "An Abstract of the Laws of New England."
2. "The Bloudy Tenant of Persecution."
3. "A Brief Exposition of the Whole Book of Canticles."
4. "A Brief Exposition with Practical Observations Upon the Whole Book of Ecclesiastes."
5. "Certain Queries Tending to Accommodation."
6. "Christ the Fountain of Life."
7. "The Correspondence of John Cotton."
8. "The Covenant of God's Free Grace."
9. "Exposition Upon the Thirteenth Chapter of Revelation."
10. "God's Mercy Mixed with His Justice."
11. "God's Promises to His Plantations." A sermon on 2 Samuel 7:10, delivered in 1630.

12. "The Grounds and Ends of the Baptism of Children."

13. "Of the Holiness of Church Members."

14. "The Keyes of the Kingdom of Heaven."

15. "The Liberty of Conscience in Matters of Religion."

16. "Milk for Babes." Appended as part of the New England Primer.

17. "The Pouring Out of the Seven Vials." An exposition of Revelation 16.

18. "A Practical Commentary or Exposition Upon the First Epistle of John."

19. "Singing of Psalmes a Gospel-Ordinance."

20. "A Treatise on the Covenant of Grace."

21. "The True Constitution of a Particular Visible Church."

22. "The Way of Life (or, God's Way and Course)."

23. "The Way of Congregational Churches Cleared."

24. "The Way of the Churches of Christ in New England."

[ORIGINAL TITLE PAGE]

SINGING
OF
PSALMS
A GOSPEL ORDINANCE
or
A TREATISE,

Where these four particulars are held:
1. Touching the duty itself.
2. Touching the matter to be sung.
3. Touching the Singers.
4. Touching the Manner of Singing

By John Cotton,
Teacher of the Church at Boston in *New England*.

LONDON,
Printed by *M.S.* for *Hannah Allen*, at the Crown in the Pope's-Head-Alley, and *John Rothwell* at the *Sun* and *Fountain* in Paul's Churchyard.
1647.

OF THE SINGING OF PSALMS CHAPTER 1:

Several Questions

"Speaking to yourselves in psalms and hymns and spiritual songs, singing and making melody in your heart to the Lord," (Eph. 5:19).

To prevent the godly minded from making melody to the Lord in singing his praises with one accord (I mean with one heart, and one voice), Satan has mightily stirred himself to breed discord in the hearts of some by filling their heads with four questions about that duty.

1. Touching on the duty itself of singing psalms with a lively voice, whether there is any such worship at all now to be allowed and practiced in the days of the New Testament. Whether the Psalms may be sung, in a manner devised, in tunes invented, or in order, after the reading of it? 2. Touching the matter to be sung, whether Scriptural psalms penned by David, Asaph, Moses, Solomon, Hezekiah, Habakkuk, Zachariah, Simeon, Deborah, Mary, Elizabeth, or the like; or songs immediately created by some personal spiritual gift of some officer or member of the church? 3. Touching on the

Chapter 1: Several Questions

singers, if vocal singing may be allowed. Who must sing? 1) Whether one person or all the rest, the rest only saying *AMEN*, or the whole congregation? 2) Whether women as well as men, or just men alone? 3) Whether carnal men and pagans, as well as church members and Christians? 4) Touching on the manner of singings, whether the psalms may be sung either, 1) in devised meter? 2) in tunes invented? 3) in order, after its reading?

For the first question, we lay down this conclusion for a doctrine of truth, "that singing of psalms with a lively voice is *a holy duty* of God's worship now in the days of the New Testament." When we say, singing with a lively voices, we assume that no one will misconstrue us, as to think we exclude singing with the heart, for God is a spirit. And to worship him with the voice without the spirit, were but lip-labor. Which, being rested is, only *lost labor*, (as is said in Isaiah 29:13), or at most, profits only a little. But this, we say, as we are to make melody in our hearts, so with our voices we are to do this also. In opposition to this, there are some anti-psalmists, who do not acknowledge any singing at all with the voice in the New Testament, but only spiritual songs of joy and comfort in the heart of the word of Christ.

First, the proof for the truth. The first proof for the truth is taken from the commandment of the Lord by Paul, who instructs and exhorts the Ephesians, to "be like one to another in Psalms and Hymns and spiritual songs," (Ephesians 5:19). And also to "teach and admonish one another in Psalms and Hymns," (Colossians 3:16), which *cannot* be done without a lively voice. The Apostle commanded the Church of Corinth, "That such as sing in the Church, should not only sing in the Spirit, but with understanding also," (1 Corinthians 14:15-16). That is, not only with their own understanding of the hearers, so that he that occupied the place of the unlearned, might be edified, and say, *amen*, at such giving of thanks. Where it follows unavoidably, that singing of Psalms is not only a making of melody to the Lord with inward grace in the heart, but *also* with a lively and audible voice, which is the point in question.

Objection 1: This place in Corinth makes nothing to the cause in hand, for these Corinthian Psalms were not the Psalms of David, or sung by the whole congregation much less in meter and tunes devised by men, as ours are, but they were spiritual songs, immediately inspired and recited by the Holy Spirit, and sung only by him who received that gift, as the Spirit gave him utterance.

Answer: We did not allege that place to prove that the singing of David's Psalms by the whole congregation in the same manner in meter and tunes as our current psalms are set

Chapter 1: Several Questions

in. All these points belong to the other questions, which will be handled later, God willing, in their place. But to this purpose we believe, "that singing of Psalms in the New Testament, is to be dispensed in Christian Churches, not only with inward grace in the heart, making melody to the Lord, but also with an outward audible lively voice." (*cf.* 1 Cor. 14:15-16). Which is the very point in hand, and which this commandment of the apostle clearly demonstrates.

Objection 2: The Apostle, to the Ephesians and Colossians, does not say *sing* to one another in Psalms, but *speak or preach* one to another, or in other words, "teach and admonish one another." The Psalms dwelling in their hearts, they were to dispense them in a way of teaching and admonishing. But as for singing, he makes no mention of that, until he came to teach them the manner of dispensing the words of Christ to God in the end of the verse. And then indeed he teaches them to sing in the Spirit, to make melody with grace in the heart to God.

Answer: Some tremble at the word, as the framer of this objection professes himself to tremble, they should rather bow their judgment's and practice to Scripture and language, then bow the sense of Scripture. It is one thing, to speak one to another in psalms, and hymns, and spiritual songs, as is done in singing, another thing to preach and teach one to another, out of psalms, and hymns, and spiritual songs. It is true, they were to teach and admonish one another *out* of the Psalms, and the scope of Paul will reach that. But if Paul had *only* meant that, in other words, that they should teach and preach one to another out of the Psalms, he would not have said, *speak you one to another in Psalms, or with Psalms*. But *out* of the Psalms, or *from* the Psalms, for such is the language of the Holy Spirit in expressing such a duty. Paul is said to have expounded, and testified, and persuaded the Jews out of the Law of Moses, and out of the Prophets, Phillip is said to begin to preach Jesus to the Eunuch, ἀπὸ τῆς γραφῆς ταύτης, from that Scripture in Isaiah, or at that Scripture in Acts 8:35. He did not preach Jesus to him in speaking that scripture.

Objection 3: If that speaking of the Ephesians one to another in Psalms, did not hold forth their expounding and preaching the psalms one to another, by only the bare reading or singing the letter of the Psalms, this was such a service where there is nothing of Christ held forth externally. I do not speak of the matter of the Psalms, but o the outward manner of dispensing it. There is nothing held forth in the singing of it after the usual manner, but what nature and art may attain to; there is no exercise of any spiritual gift held forth in it, as is in all other administrations, which Christ has ordained. 2. Besides, as such a singing is not a gift of Christ, so neither

Chapter 1: Several Questions

does it tend to the glory of Christ. The church not edified by itself when a pagan singing with us, might edify the Church. 3. From both of these, is appears that such singing of Psalms tends to the dishonor of Christ. Seeing it holds forth externally no more, then what a carnal man, indeed a pagan might express.

Answer 1: Singing of Psalms holds forth as much of Christ externally, as the reading of the word, or as the hearing of it read or preached, or as the falling down on our knees in prayer, and saying amen in the end of it. For though the word, when it is publicly read, ought to also be opened after the reading, yet the very reading of it, is itself an ordinance, and is not without a blessing to the faithful reader or hearer of it, no more than other ordinances or else there would be some ordinances of God like to human ceremonies, empty and beggarly.

Answer 2: Moral duties, even in pagans, may edify the Church as Abimelech's reproofs of Abraham and Sarah.

Answer 3: Singing of Psalms is accompanied and blessed of God, with many gracious effects, above nature or art, as 1. It allays the passions of melancholy and choler, indeed and scatters the furious temptations of evil spirits (1 Sam. 16:23), where it also helps to assuage enmity, and to restore friendship and favor, as in Saul to David. It was not the sound of David's harp that could have this power, either over the evil spirit, or over the sinful passions of Saul himself, if the sound of the harp had not been quickened and lively, as it were by a spiritual song, and by the Spirit of God breathing in it.

2. Singing of a spiritual song, prepares to prophecy, by ministering the spirit, "Whilest the Minstrel played, the hand of the Lord," that is his spirit, "came upon Elisha," (2 Kings 3:15). The minstrel's playing, if it had not been accompanied with a spiritual song, it could not have conveyed such a spiritual blessing. They could have been said to have prophesied with harps and viols, unless they had sung some holy songs, together with their playing on instruments. For prophecy is an utterance only of the word of God, and of the things of God contained in it, which instruments without voice cannot do. Nor had their playing with instruments been a means of conveying the spirit to Saul, had not their voices concurred and sung with their instruments.

3. Singing of Psalms honors God with our glory (Psalm 108:3, and 57:7-8). Where David's glory being distinguished not only from his harp, but from his heart, it cannot fitly be understood of any other member, but his tongue, by which he was accustomed in singing to glorify God.

Objection 4: These gracious effects and fruits of singing Psalms, do plead as much for singing and playing with instruments, as for singing with voices.

Chapter 1: Several Questions

Answer 1: This last effect of singing to the glory of God with our glory, is peculiar only to singing with our mouths.

Answer 2: Suppose it were true that these effects of singing Psalms pleaded as much for singing and playing with instruments, as singing with voices, yet it is evident, that singing with voices had the preeminence, as that which uttering the word of God, chiefly uttered the Spirit of God breathing in it. And with all evidence it is likewise, that it is no impeachment to an ordinance, that the outward dispensing of it may be performed by nature and art, but notwithstanding that it may be accompanied of God with a spiritual blessing.

Answer 3: Singing with instruments, was typical and was a ceremonial worship, and therefore is ceased. But singing with the heart and voice is a moral worship, such as is written in the hearts of all men by nature. As to pray in distress, so when we are merry, and have cause of solemn thanksgiving to God, then to sing Psalms, which the Holy Spirit by the Apostle James approves and sanctifies this in James 5:13. Or suppose singing with instruments were not typical, but only an external solemnity of worship, fitted to the solace of the outward fences of children under age, (such as the Israelites were under the Old Testament (Galatians 4:1-3), yet now in the grown age of the heirs of the New Testament, such external pompous solemnities are stopped, and no external worship reserved, but such as holds forth simplicity, and gravity, neither is any voice now to be heard in the Church of Christ, but such as is significant and edifying by his signification (1 Cor. 14:10, 11, 26), which the voice of instruments is not.

Answer 4: It is an honor to Christ, and to his grace, not only when we hold spiritual gifts, but also when we perform Christian duties. And duties performed in faith, (which without prayer itself is not accepted), they do not go without a spiritual blessing, although nature and art might perform the same for the outward work. The trailing of the weapons of the Israelites, and their military march, both in silence and shouting, about the walls of Jericho (Joshua 6:13-20), was no greater work externally, then carnal men and pagans might have performed as well as Israelites, but this being done by Israelites in faith and obedience to God's command, it was mighty through God to cast down the high and strong walls of Jericho. And the Apostle looks at this and the like precedents, sets forth faith as that which is prevalent and effectual in both testaments, howsoever the work or worship is external (Heb. 11:30). In like manner it is with the reading of the word, and the hearing of it, as also the silent joining in prayer, and concluding it with *amen*, though all these are such duties as nature and art may perform the outward work of them. Yet when the people of God perform the same in the faith of Christ, and in the obedience of God's command, they find a gracious blessing of God. Indeed, carnal and profane people and pagans, although they cannot expect the same blessing from their empty outside performances, yet they sometimes taste more sweetness and enlargement there, than flesh and blood could imagine, in 1 Samuel 10:5-6, Saul joining with the prophets in their holy melody found another spirit coming on him, which also argues that they joined a profane and carnal *hypocrite*

Objection 5: It may be in the Old Testament, as well as in the new, God did not allow or bless any worship as nature and art could accomplish, as some might believe are allowed and blessed of God in the old administration. But now in the New Testament, as God is a spirit, so he allows and blesses *no* worship, but what is dispensed in Spirit and truth.

Answer 1: God was a spirit in the Old Testament, as well as in the new, and he did not allow and bless any worship but what was either performed in spirit and truth, or conveyed spirit and truth. Albeit more external rites in worship were then appointed, then in the New Testament are now continued, for which end Christ alleges those words in the place in John, to which you allude. But nevertheless, though Christ has not limited his worship to any certain place now, as then (which was the point that Christ spoke about), and neither does he rest in external performance, however evident it is, God has appointed in these days of the Gospel sundry external worship now as well as then, (and the same in both Testaments to be performed in *spirit and truth*), as hearing and reading the word, kneeling in prayer, and saying, amen, all which nature and art may perform as the singing of Psalms with vocal melody.

CHAPTER 2:

Propounding and clearing the second proof for singing Psalms with a lively voice.

The second proof is taken from the examples of Christ himself, and of his Saints and Disciples in the New Testament. Christ Himself, with his disciples, sung a Psalm or a hymn together, in the end of the administration of the Lord's Supper in Matthew 26:30. And Paul and Silas are said to have "sung a Psalm in the prison, so as the prisoners heard them," (Acts 16:25). Now, if in singing they had only spiritually rejoiced, and not expressed their joy, and their song in an audible and lively voice, the prisoners could not have heard them. The stranger does not know or meddle with the spiritual joy of the heart, which is said in Proverbs 14:10.

Objection 1: The place in Matthew 26:30 may as well be translated, "They prayed to God, as they sung an hymn."

Answer: Though the meaning is, *they praised God*, yet the word implies that they praised God with a Hymn, for it is improper in that language to translate the word "praise" (whether God or man) but either with a song, or with a poem. It is more probable, then any reason can show, that Christ and his Disciples ended the Lord's Supper with singing one of their Hebrew Psalms, as the Jews were accustomed to end their celebration of that Passover (as their own records tell us) with singing Psalms with the five other Psalms next following together. But all that I now intend, is to show that Christ and his Disciples sang together, and therefore with their voices as well as their hearts.

Objection 2: They might be said to sing together, if one alone sang and the rest said amen, in the end. As men may be said to pray together, where one alone speaks, and the rest consent.

Answer: This is true, but then one at least speaks with an audible and lively voice, though the rest does not. And that is enough to clear the point in hand, that singing in the New Testament, consists not only in making melody with grace in the heart, but also in singing to the Lord with a lively voice.

Answer 2: If the disciples did not join in singing that hymn, but only by silent consent, they might as well be said, to have taken the bread, blessed it, broken it, and distributed it (with the wine as well), for all this Christ did with their silent consent. But what Christ did alone is expressly recorded, as done by himself. When it comes to the singing of the Psalms, that is recorded as done by them in the plural number, "When they had sung a hymn, they departed into the Mount of Olives," (Matt. 26:30). They that departed into the Mount of Olives, they sung the Psalm. Now it was not Christ alone, but the whole eleven disciples with him that departed into the Mount of Olives. And therefore it was Christ with his disciples who sung the Psalm together.

Objection 3: Against the proof from Acts 16:25. It is not said, (as some say), that Paul and Silas sung the Psalms of David or Asaph, much less with meter and tunes devised by men. Had they done so, the prisoners that heard them might have sung, for the outward dispensation, such a song of praise to God, as well as they.

Answer: We do not allege this example of theirs (as has been often said in like case before), to prove that they sang any Psalm of David, though it stands with good reason, that they joining together in singing, did rather sing a Psalm (or Hymn) known to them both, then any new song devised by either of them, but what Psalms are to be sung is another question, which with the help of Christ, we will speak to in the sequel. Neither do we allege their example to prove, they sang in a devised meter or tune. For they being Hebrews, it is likely that they sang the Hebrew songs in the tunes of the Sanctuary, but that also is another question, of which we are to speak in this place, when we come to it. All that we gather from this place now is no more than the words plainly hold forth, that they sung a hymn to God, not only with inward melody of grace in their hearts, but also with an outward melody of the voice, for else the prisoners could not have heard them.

"Against this, it is of no force to object, as some do, that if they had sung any of the Psalms of David or Asaph with an audible voice, then the other prisoners also might have joined with them, and have worshipped (outwardly at least) as well as they."

For the answer is plain and ready. First, the prison was in Philippi, a city in Macedonia, consisting partly of a colony of the Romans, partly of the Grecians, and no Jews were mentioned to be inhabitants there, much less prisoners at that time. And for pagans to join in singing Hebrew songs, in Hebrew verses and tunes, it seems to be far beyond either their skill or devotion. Secondly, suppose the prisoners had been Jews (of which there is no hint at all in the text) and suppose that those prisoners who were hearing the melody of Paul and Silas, and knowing the song, had joined in the outward singing of it, and that without any grace in their hearts (none of all which things appear in the story), yet suppose all this, will the unbelief of those Jews make the holy worship of these Apostles, and their faith to God, or the faith to God to them, of none effect? Paul renounces and abhors such carnal reason, as we see in Romans 3:3.

CHAPTER 3:

Propounding and clearing the third proof, for singing Psalms with a lively voice.

A third proof of this truth is "taken from the prophecies of the old testament, foretelling and persuading such a duty in the New," (Isaiah 52:8), with the voice together they will sing. And that is foretold of the time "when the seat of the messenger of glad tidings shall be beautiful, who shall say unto Zion, Thy God reigneth," Which Paul explains of the times of the Gospel, (Romans 10:14). "Make a joyful noise unto the Lord all ye Lands. Come before his presence with singing," (Psalm 100:1-2). *All you lands*, implies the nations of the Gentiles, as well as of the Jews, which pertains to the times of the New Testament, so that now all are exhorted to sing before the presence of God, with a loud noise or voice.

"O come, let us sing unto the Lord. Let us make a joyful noise to the rock of our salvation. Let us make a joyful noise unto him with Psalms," (Psalm 95:1-2). Which Psalms the Apostle himself interprets to be meant of the times of the gospel. Which is the more to be observed, because the Psalmist, exhorting to the holy and reverent performance of the ordinary duties of the Sabbath, he mentions first thanksgiving in singing of Psalms with a loud voice, and the reasons of it (verses 1-5). And then solemn prayer with the reasons of it (verses 6-7), and then faithful attention to the preaching of the Word on that day, not hardening their hearts against it, through unbelief (verses 7-8), so the end of our passage says, "Today if ye will hear his voice, harden not your hearts," (Psalm 95:7,8,11). And today, the Apostle interprets it to be meant not of the seventh day of rest from the creation, nor of the day of rest, where Joshua gave the people inheritance and rest in Canaan, but of the day of rest in the New Testament (Heb. 4:3-9). Where the Apostle infers, that there is remaining to us another Sabbath, or day of rest, now in the days of the Gospel, different from the seventh day of rest, kept in regard of God's rest from Creation, and different from the day of rest in Joshua's time. But the day of rest remaining to us, he declares to be that day where our Lord Jesus entered into his rest. And that was our Lord's Day, which David foretold should be celebrated with solemn prayer, preaching and hearing the word, and singing of Psalms, and that with a joyful noise.

Objection 1: Although David exhorts all lands to sing to the Lord with a loud noise, it does not appear that we should make such a manner of loud noise, as our singing is, no more than such a loud noise, as was made in David's days, with ten stringed instruments, for so the Lord was to be praised. I acknowledge from these texts, that it is the duty of all those who are called to the knowledge of the truth, when they come before the Lord, not to come before him with sorrow and sadness, and with a dejected spirit, but with *singing*, or else, they dishonor the Lord Jesus, the spiritual chief singer, Author of their new song. But although this prophecy foretells of the joyful approaching of the spiritual worshippers before the Lord, yet it binds them no more to make such a noise, as the singing book teaches, that the trees are to clap their hands, as Isaiah prophesizes, or as the new converts are bound to come with external singing, when they come to join themselves with the Church, as in Isaiah 51:11. And as for such a manner of noise, as is made in our mixed assemblies, the Psalm speaks nothing to it.

Answer: You see, the manner of noise which is made by singing in our assemblies does not pertain to the present question in hand. And therefore we refer it to the sequel. The question now, is whether in the days of the New Testament, we are to sing the praises of God, with a loud voice, or noise. And for this we say, besides the text in Isaiah, the prophecies of David, who foretell and exhort all lands (at least the churches and people of God in all lands) "To make a joyful noise unto the Lord, to make a joyful noise unto him with Psalms, to come before his presence with singing," (Psalm 100:1-2 and Psalm 95:1-2).

Objection 2: Indeed, but this no longer binds us to make such a manner of loud noise, as our form of singing is, then to make such a loud noise, as was made in David's days, with ten stringed instruments, for so the Lord was to be praised.

Answer: So the Lord was to be praised, praised with ten stringed instruments. When was he to be praised as such? In the days of David? True, and therefore it was the duty of all people in any land, that became proselytes to the Church of Israel in the days of David, and during all the time of the temple worship, to come before the Lord, not only with the loud noise of singing Psalms, but of playing with Instruments. But after the days, not only of David, but of the Temple, and that worship that is past, in the day when our Jehovah (the Lord Jesus) has entered into his rest, in the day of our Lord, when he commands us not to harden our hearts, but to hear his voice, to fall down and worship before him in prayer, (both which are to be performed every Lord's Day), he then commands us to "come and sing unto the Lord, to make a joyful noise to the rock of our salvation, and to make a joyful noise to him with Psalms," (Psalm 95:1-2). Here is now no mention of making a joyful noise with instruments, but with *Psalms*. And therefore the making of joyful noise with Psalms still continues, even on our Lord's days, when making a joyful noise with instruments does not continue, but is laid down in silence. Save only so far as it is kept alive in the anti-type, the

Chapter 3: Singing with a Lively Voice, Proofs

affections of our hearts, (our *Precordia*) making melody with the songs and professions of our lips, and with the gracious and peaceable conversation of our lives.

It is said, "When you acknowledge it to be the duty of such as are called to the knowledge of the truth to come before the Lord, not with sorrow and sadness, and with a dejected spirit, but with singing."

What singing do you mean? If you mean only the gracious rejoicing of the heart, that indeed, though it is requisite to avoid hypocrisy, it is not yet complete to reach the full extent of our duty, the duty of making a joyful noise with Psalms. Our chief *Singer* (Christ, of whom you speak), when he set the Lord, and his own death and resurrection before his face, (which he was to undergo for our sakes), he was not only glad in his heart, but his glory also. That is, with his tongue he rejoiced in singing a Psalm at his last supper. And therefore it will be a discord from the practice of our chief singer, and so a dishonor to him, if our hearts sing with joy, but our glory (in other words, our tongues) are mute with silence. Do not say, as you do, "We are no more bound to make a loud noise with our voices, then the trees are to clap their hands, as Isaiah prophecies, or when the new converts were to come with external singing of Psalms," (Isaiah 51:11?)

For in saying that, you will not need to avoid the authority of the commandment, neither the necessity of that duty of singing. For when God redeemed his people out of the captivity of Babel, not only their hearts were filled with rejoicing, but even their tongues also with singing. And although the trees cannot be said in proper speech to clap their hands (for they have no hands to clap), yet common sense will easily tell you that there is a metaphor, either in clapping hands is described by a metaphor, for the flourishing fruitfulness of the trees of the field, which (by the blessing of God) is accustomed to follow the prosperity of the Church; in such abundance, that their boughs and branches will clap and dash themselves and their fruit one upon another. They reach forth refreshing and being food for the children of the Church. But if trees are put by a metaphor for trees of righteousness, then they will "clap their hands, and shout for joy, and sing aloud to behold and consider the wonderful goodness of the Lord," (Isaiah 55:12). And so, in the same verse, when the mountains and hills are said to break forth before the saints into singing, if there is not a metaphor in singing, then mountains and hills are put, metaphorically, for princes and men of high degree (Psalm 72:3) which will give example to others in holy rejoicing, and particularly in singing praises to the Lord. So that these texts in Isaiah, which you thought might excuse you from singing with the voice (which David exhorted to be done with a *loud* voice), they will not exempt you at all from this duty, but rather bind you the stronger to

Chapter 3: Singing with a Lively Voice, Proofs

it. And therefore look, as when David says, "I cried to the Lord with my voice," (Psalm 3:4 and 77:1). A man will detract from his meaning that will say, he cried only to God with his heart. So when David exhorted the Gentile Churches, to make a joyful noise to God with Psalms, you detract in the same way from his meaning, when you make his meaning to be, not that we should sing to God with our voices, but that we should only make melody to him, with grace in our hearts. Such detracting from the word is alike disallowed, and accursed of God, as is adding to the word.

Objection 3: Singing of Psalms of it as a *type*; neither does any evidence of reason to declare it.

1. You might as well say, that praying with the voice was a type of praying with the heart, and so is now abolished.

2. If singing of Psalms with a loud noise, had been a typical worship, David would not have exhorted us to the practice of it on the Lord's Day of the New Testament. (Psalm 95: 1-2 and 7).

3. Christ and his Apostles would not have used it in the Lord's Supper, which is a feast of the New Testament, (Matthew 26:30), neither would Paul and Silas have used it in prison among the Gentiles, (Acts 16:25).

4. The light of nature, which is never accustomed to teach us types and shadows, does as well teach us to praise

God in singing with our tongues, in time of our rejoicing as to cry to God with our voices in times of our distress.

CHAPTER 4:

Propounding the Second Question, stating and proving it.

The second question about the singing of Psalms, concerns the matter of the Psalms to be sung, for there are some who do not scruple singing with the voices, but singing the Psalms of David now in the days of the New Testament. As conceiving that David's Psalms were penned for temple worship, during the pedagogy of the Old Testament. But now in the days of the New Testament, when God has promised to pour out his Spirit on all flesh, now the whole worship of God should be carried on, not by set forms of Psalms (no more then by set forms of prayer), but by personal spiritual gifts, by which someone or other of the members of the Church, having received a Psalm by the entitlement of the spirit, he sings it openly in the public assembly of the Church, and the rest of the brethren say *amen* to it in the close.

But touching the persons of those who should sing, it pertains to the third question. This second question chiefly concerns the matter to be sung, whether the Psalms of David, or some Psalm, or Hymn, indicated by the personal gift of this or that member of the Church. Where we hold and believe:

1. That not only the Psalms of David, but any other spiritual songs recorded in Scripture, may lawfully be sung in Christian Churches, as the song of Moses, and Asaph, Heman

and Ethan, Solomon and Hezekiah, Habakkuk and Zachary, Hannah and Deborah, Mary and Elizabeth, and the like.

2. We grant as well, that any private Christian, who has a gift to frame a spiritual song, may both frame it and sing it privately, for his own private comfort, and remembrance of some special benefit, or deliverance. Neither do we forbid the private use of an instrument of music with it, so that attention to the instrument does not divert the heart from attention to the matter of the song.

Neither do we deny, but that in the public thanksgivings of the Church, if the Lord should furnish any of the members of the Church with a spiritual gift to compose a Psalm on any special occasion, he may lawfully be allowed to sing it before the Church, and the rest hearing it, and approving it, may go along with him in Spirit, and say *amen* to it. "When Christ ascended on high," to sit on his throne of glory, looking as princes are accustomed to do in the day of their coronation, (*Spargere Missilia and Domaria*) so he poured out his gifts abundantly on all sorts, gifts of miracles, healing, tongues, *etc.* And the churches were willing, when they saw such special gifts of the Spirit poured out, to make use of them, as occasion served. Where it was, that sundry of the members of the Church of Corinth, as they had received a gift of Psalms and tongues from the Lord Jesus, so they had allowance from the Church to employ their gifts to the public edification. But as such gifts now are not ordinarily bestowed, which were at first given chiefly for admiration and conviction of Infidels as we see in 1 Corinthians 14:22, so we would not call on men now, to prefer their ordinary common gift as more fit for the public edifying of the Church, before the extraordinary gifts of the holy men of God in Scripture, who by the Spirit were guided to prepare spiritual songs, suitable to all of the conditions and affections and temptations of the Church and people of God in all ages. So then the question is, whether the Psalms of David, and Asaph, and such other hymns and spiritual songs recited by the prophets, and recorded in Scripture, are appointed by God, to be ordinarily sung in Christian Churches, or whether laying aside Scripture songs, we are to sing only such spiritual songs, as will be recited by the personal, but ordinary, gifts of any ordinary officer or member of the Church? The former we hold to be the truth, others the latter.

The reasons of our faith and practice are *these*:

1. Taken from the commandment, or exhortation of the apostle, "Be filled you with the spirit, speaking to yourselves in Psalms and Hymns and spiritual songs, singing and making melody in your hearts to the Lord," (Ephesians 5:19). To the like purpose is his commandment and exhortation to the Colossians in Chapter 3:16, "Let the word of Christ dwell in you richly, in all wisdom, teaching and admonishing one

another, in Psalms and Hymns and spiritual songs, singing with grace in your hearts to the Lord." In both places, as the apostle exhorts us to singing, so he instructs us what the matter of our song should be, in other words, Psalms, Hymns, and spiritual songs, now those three are the very titles of the songs of David, as they are delivered to us by the Holy Spirit himself. Some of them are called Psalms, some Hymns, some songs and spiritual songs (מִזְמוֹר *Mizmor*, שִׁיר *Schir*, תְּהִלָּה *Trebillim*). Now, what reason can be given why the apostle should direct us in our singing to the very titles of David's Psalms, if it were not his meaning that we should sing them? Indeed, either we must exclude the Psalms of David, from the name of psalms, hymns, and spiritual songs, or else we must be forced to acknowledge that we are exhorted to sing them, as well as any other.

CHAPTER 5:

Clearing Objections

Before we precede to any further reasons of the point let us first, by the help of Christ, clear the objections against this. The objections are many, and some of them seem more weighty, and some more light. Let us impartially and evenly, by the Lord's guidance, weigh them all in the balance of the sanctuary.

Objection: If Paul had meant David's Psalms, or Scripture-songs, it would have been an easy matter to have named David's Psalms, or Scripture-songs, as David himself named his songs, the Psalms or songs of David, when he delivered them to the chief musician, and to his company to be sung.

Answer 1: My first answer is, that it may be as justly said, that if Paul had meant to exclude David's Psalms, or Scripture-songs, it would have been as easy to have excluded them by name, and to have limited them only to such Psalms and Songs, as the spirit should suggest to their hearts.

Answer 2: My second answer is, that the apostle expresses mainly names such as psalms, hymns, and spiritual songs, and these three are the very express titles of the Psalms in the Psalm-book. Now, why he should direct them to the very titles of David's Psalms, and yet not mean the Psalms, that bear those titles, can a good conscience give a good reason for it?

Answer 3: My third answer is, that when David gave his Psalms and Songs to the musicians in Israel, it was here he should set his name to them, or by some other mark make it appear, that the Psalms were inspired and delivered by a Prophet of God. But after the book of Psalms was generally known and received to be of divine inspiration, the Psalms are as usually alleged in the New Testament, without the name of David, as with Luke 24:44, and Acts 13:33.

Objection 2: The Psalms here committed to the spiritual singers to be sung, are the words of Christ, which are to dwell richly in us, in Colossians 3:16. But the Psalms dedicated to the sons of Korah, were the words of David and Asaph. And so the Holy Spirit calls them. No, but that the words spoken are to be the spiritual songs of the Saints, where they are to teach one another, and to sing to God, they are words spoken to the heart, by the voice of the Spirit of Christ. Besides, the word of Christ is properly the Gospel, by way of eminency, in way of opposition to the Law, given by Moses.

Answer 1: The words of David and Asaph, as they were the words of Christ in the mouth of David and Asaph. So they were the words of Christ also in the mouths of the sons of Korah, or any other singers in the temple. If any of them did not sing them, others would sing the word itself or godly

Chapter 5: Clearing Objections

singers of the temple (such as Heman, Jeduthun, and others) who were spiritual, and holy men, sang them with melody in their hearts, as well as in their voices. And it will be alike a sinful defect in the New Testament, in such as sing the Psalms of David, to sing them without some measure of the Spirit of David. For the Apostle expressly requires, that we should sing with grace in our hearts. But if the words of David and Asaph, be the words of Christ, and be sung of the Church, with grace in the heart, we demand whether this act of the Church, be no an act of faith, and the obedience of faith to the word of Christ, in that text of the Apostle?

Answer 2: It is an unsafe and unsavory expression, to speak of the words of David and Asaph, as if they were only the words of Christ in the mouths of Spiritual Singers. For if they were not the words of Christ in the mouths of carnal singers also, then the holy Scriptures were not the word of Christ, if they are read by a carnal reader. So the unbelief of man will make the faith of God of no effect, indeed the word of God, not to be the word of God.

Answer 3: Let it be considered in the fear of God, whether the words of Asaph or David, sung with grace in the heart to God, be not as truly and properly (in the Apostles sense) the word of Christ, as any song recited by the private gift of any saint of God now living? If so, then the Apostle encourages us to sing the Psalms of David and Asaph with their spirit. If not, then there are Christians now that are carried by a more infallible spirit then the prophets were in old time. And yet Paul speaks of the Saints now, as led by the spirit of God in Romans 8:14. But Peter speaks of the prophets then, as carried by the Holy Spirit in 2 Peter 1:21; which puts this difference, that such as are led by the Spirit may err, but such as are carried by the Spirit, are carried and lifted above themselves by the Holy Spirit, and *cannot err*. And so were David and Asaph.

Answer 4: Although the words of Christ are the gospel, yet the words of David are not to be shut out of the Gospel, for the Gospel was preached to Israel, when David and the other Prophets were preached, indeed, and some parts of Moses.

Objection 3: But, if the Apostle had intended to commend to the Churches the singing of the psalms and hymns, and spiritual songs of David and Asaph, what need was there for him to exhort either the "Ephesians to be filled with the Spirit," or to the Colossians, "to have the word of Christ dwell richly in them," for such a service? For any small measure of the Spirit, and of the Word, will suffice to sing the Psalms of David and Asaph, in their words, and in the meter and tunes accustomed. But to invent new spiritual songs, fit to teach and admonish in the Church, would require a full measure of the Spirit, and a rich treasure of the word to dwell in us. And therefore Paul bids the Ephesians to be filled with

Chapter 5: Clearing Objections

the Spirit, in singing the spiritual songs of the New Testament, as drunkards are filled with wine, and in the strength and spirits of their wine, invent and sing their wanton sonnets.

Answer 1: My first answer is that Paul exhorted them to be filled with the Spirit, as drunkards are with wine, not that they might invent, and sing spiritual songs, as drunkards do wanton sonnets, for neither do drunkards filled with wine, usually invent sonnets, but sing such as they learned before, when they were sober, and neither does the Apostle speak of inventing songs at all, either wanton songs by drunkards, or spiritual songs by the Faithful, but only to be filled with the Spirit, as drunkards are with wine, so that they might avoid the riotous and excessive mirth of drunkards, and employ and improve their holy mirth and joy, to the singing of psalms and hymns and spiritual songs, for their own mutual edification and consolation, and for holy thanksgiving and praise to the Lord.

Answer 2: My second answer is that, although it does not require such a full measure of the spirit, or rich portion of the word dwelling in us, to sing a psalm invented and penned to our hands. Yet a full and rich measure of the Word and Spirit will be needful to perform all of those duties, which the Apostle in those texts calls for. For the Apostle calls to the improvement, as of the whole word of Christ, to the teaching and admonishing of one another, so of the Psalms, not only to those two heads, but also besides those, to a further third end, in other words, to the singing of them to God's praise. Now to be able to improve the whole word of God to these two spiritual ends and the Psalms to all those three spiritual ends does require a full and rich measure both of the Spirit and the word dwelling in us.

Answer 3: My third answer is that, it will require a full and rich measure both of the word and Spirit to dwell in us, to direct and appoint a fit Psalm, (out of the Book of Psalms), suitable to the present occasions of singing to God's praise, and to the instruction and admonition of the Church, according to the present estate of their affections, or afflictions, their consolation, or conversation in hand.

Answer 4: My *fourth* answer is that, it will require a fuller and richer measure of the Word and Spirit to dwell in us, then a carnal heart would imagine even to utter a song with such grace in the heart, as a mighty melody to the Lord, it requires a good measure of the indwelling Spirit, and word of God to pray in the Spirit, but much more to sing in the spirit, where our senses delighted with the melody are apt to steal away our hearts from the spiritual fervency. Deborah found her heart dull, and needing to be awakened, so much as to utter the song, which she had prepared by the Spirit for her and Barak to sing together in Judges 5:12. "Awake, Awake,

Chapter 5: Clearing Objections

Awake, Awake Deborah, utter a song." That fourfold ingemination argues in the best of God's servants, a deep drowsiness of spirit, when we should come to utter a spiritual song spiritually. Like that fourfold ingemination to the Church of Jerusalem, to return, return, return, return, (Song of Songs 6:13). So that argues a deep and strong averseness of the spirit of the Jews to conversion, and returning to the Lord.

Objection 4: The Apostle calls the whole word of Christ dwelling in us, psalms and hymns and Spiritual Songs, neither does he limit us to one prophet more then to another, unless you will say, that the words of Christ in the Gospel, or which was prophesied by the rest of the Prophets, were not spiritual songs. But the Apostle calls them all "psalms and hymns and spiritual Songs," as well as David's, if they dwell in the heart. For the words of Christ there, (in other words, *in the heart*) are songs for the spirit, or else they are no songs to any man. Therefore as yet, to sing the prophecies of David after our common manner is not worship commanded or taught to us in holy writ.

My first answer to this is that it is a groundless assertion to say, that Paul calls the whole word of God dwelling in us, psalms and hymns and spiritual songs. For why then should the Holy Spirit give that style and title of psalms and hymns and spirituals songs only to the book of Psalms, and to none else of all the books of the prophets or apostles? Again, if Paul called the words of all the Prophets, psalms and hymns and spiritual songs, why then did not the prophets in their own language pen them with musical accents, as well as the Psalms of David and Asaph.

Besides, if the words of all the prophets were spiritual songs, why then did the Prophets themselves find the books of their own prophecies bitter in their bellies? There are many words of the Prophets, that are more fit matter for humiliation and mourning before the Lord, then fit to be sung as spiritual songs to the Lord. But suppose that there are many words of Christ, and his prophets, that are fit matter for spiritual rejoicing (as indeed all the doctrines and promises of Grace be), yet what warrant have we to sing them, as in some cathedral churches and colleges, the Bible clerks do sing their chapters out of the Old and New Testament?

Answer 2: My second answer is that whether the words of Christ in the Gospel, or in the Prophets, are spiritual songs or not, yet if the Psalms of David are also the words of Christ, if they likewise dwell in our hearts, and if they are spiritual songs too, then it will unavoidably follow, that the same word of the Apostle that commands us to sing psalms and hymns and Spiritual Songs, commands us also to sing the Psalms of David and Asaph to the Lord, unless you will say, that the Psalms of David and Asaph (although dwelling in the heart), are neither Psalms or Hymns or Spiritual Songs, howsoever

Chapter 5: Clearing Objections

the Holy Spirit entities them by such names. How then can you say, "That to sing the prophecies of David, does not yet appear to be our common manner of singing of them, we shall have occasion to speak to that hereafter."

Objection 5: David's Psalms, considered, not as Scriptures divinely inspired, but as spiritual songs seem to be appropriated to the Temple worship. One, because they are appointed to be sung by proper officers and musical instruments, belonging to the Temple, as appears by the titles of several Psalms. Two, because neither Christ, or the Apostles in their writings, used them at all, otherwise then as the other writings of Moses, and the Prophets, for instruction and illustration, teaching us how to use the same. Those Psalms therefore as songs, being proper to that service of the temple, are abolished with the temple worship.

Answer 1: My first answer to this argument is that both of these reasons are too slender to confine that David's Psalms were appointed to be sung by the officers and musical instruments of the Temple, yet not above one part of three, considering the length of Psalm 119. There are a hundred and fifty Psalms in all, and all of these not above 57 are appointed to be sung by the officers and musical instruments of the Temple, yet not above one part of three are free from any express reference to the Temple.

Answer 2: My second answer is that the matter of some Psalms does evidently argue, they were not appointed to be sung always in the Temple, or at least did agree more properly to other times then those, where the temple stood. The 74th Psalm (which was a Psalm of Asaph, but joined with the Psalms of David) complained that the enemies had sent God's sanctuary into the fire, (as the Hebrew words are) and had defiled it by casting down the dwelling place of his name to the ground. The 44th Psalm, although it was committed to the sons of Korah, yet surely it was chiefly intended (as Paul applies part of it), to the item of the New Testament, for I suppose that it could never be verified of any times in the Jewish Temple that God gave up the people of Israel as sheep for meat, to be killed all the day, to be appointed for the slaughter, before broken in the place of dragons, and covered with the shadow of death, when as yet though all this evil had come upon them, they had not forgotten their God, or dealt falsely in his covenant, or in their hearts turned back, nor their steps declined from his way. Paul acknowledges this very word to be accomplished in the Saints of the primitive churches in the Apostle's times, but where will we find the like innocence, when the same calamity met together in the children of Israel, while the temple was standing? And is it credible, this Psalm was confined to be sung in the Temple, where they could not sing it, but with a sad reproof to

Chapter 5: Clearing Objections

themselves for their discord in practice, and yet forbidden to be sung in the churches of the New Testament, where they might sing it, both to hear, and sing, and practice, all of them keeping holy consent and harmony together?

Answer 3: My third answer is that it appears by the titles of such Psalms as are directed to the officers and instruments of Temple-music, that there was something typical or rudimental in the manner of singing some of the Psalms of David and Asaph in the Temple worship. But this does not argue any more, that the whole service of God in singing David's Psalms was typical or rudimental, then it will argue prayer to be a typical and Temple worship, because prayer in the Temple was offered with incense, and so with the Temple and with the incense to be abolished. He that will make the Psalms of David to be *types* of the spiritual songs of the New Testament, therefore, now, abolishes them to be sung. He might as well say that the letters in the Scriptures of the Old Testament were typical and so abolishable reading of the Holy Scriptures now in the days of the New Testament.

Answer 4: My fourth answer is that it has been showed above, that singing of Psalms with a lively voice, is not a ceremonial but a moral duty, and so continues now in the days of the New Testament, so it may be as truly said, that the singing of David's Psalms, and other Scripture-songs, is in like sort not a ceremonial but a moral duty, and so of the same continuance in the New Testament. The Psalms of David and Asaph, and the rest, are as full of holy and lively, spiritual, and evangelical meditations and affections, instruments, prayers, and praises, as any that we can expect to be endited by any officer or member of the Christian Churches now. Indeed, it is to be feared that the Psalms compiled by the most devout Christians now, would fall short of those of David and Asaph, ceremonial types of the spiritual songs of the faithful in the New Testament, when as types are accustomed to be more carnal, and worldly, and literal, and less spiritual and lively, then the antitypes. But here the anti-types are less spiritual and lively then the types.

Answer 5: As a final answer, for that other reason take from the practice of Christ and his apostles, in their writings never used the Psalms of David for spiritual songs, as the writings of Moses and other Prophets for instruction and illustration, this is of as small force as the former.

1. Firstly, writings are not a place or reason for the use of spiritual songs. Psalms are to be used for songs in Church Assemblies, and private soliloquies and conferences, not in writings. And yet so far as the Psalms may be used to the Ephesians and Colossians, where he instructs both churches, and in them all others, to sing these psalms, hymns, and spiritual songs. Among which these Psalms of David and

Chapter 5: Clearing Objections

Asaph, if they are not principally intended, yet surely they are plainly included, or else they are neither the word of Christ, and neither are they psalms and hymns and spiritual songs.

2. Secondly, it is not credible that Christ never used the Psalms of David and Asaph for spiritual songs. For the use of those Psalms for songs was doubtlessly a part of God's worship, which was then in force, how then, did he say, "That it became him to fulfill all righteousness," (Matthew 3:15).

Besides, many things that Jesus did and said were not written in the gospels, Acts, or the Epistles. And yet this is said that he with his disciples sung a Hymn (Matthew 26:30). And Hymns are the general title for the whole book of Psalms, for although it is translated, "The Book of Psalms," everyone that knows that language, knows that the word is, "the Book of Hymns." So that looks, like as when in ordinary speech we say "They sung a Psalm," we mean of a Psalm or David or Asaph, because such are not to be sung in ordinary use. So when the Evangelist says, Christ and his Disciples sung a Hymn, the people of God would not easily understand any other but one or more of David's Hymns, because they were accustomed to be the ordinary songs used in the worship of God. And surely if Christ and his Disciples had sung any other Hymn, then one of these Psalms of David and Asaph, which were accustomed to be sung in their Temples and Synagogues, the Evangelists who are accustomed to record far less matters in things which pertain to God's worship, they would not have omitted the substituting of a Hymn accustomed to be sung at the end of the Passover.

The same may be said of Paul and Silas, who are recorded (Acts 16:25) to have sung a hymn to God, where common understanding would take it for one or more of the hymns of David or Asaph, and not any other new invented spiritual song, unless some hint in the text might carry us from the ordinary meaning and use of the word among the people of God.

Objection 6: We are called upon by David himself to sing new songs (Psalm 96:1), and often elsewhere, and such as had gifts then used them for reciting and singing new songs, as Asaph, Haman, Ethan, and the four beasts (Revelation 5:9) and the 144,000 followers of the Lamb sang a new song, as did they also, who had gotten victory over the beast (Revelation 15:3-4).

Answer 1: To this, my first answer is that there is no estate and condition that ever befell the church and people of God, or can befall them, but the Holy Spirit, as he did foresee the same, for he has provided and recorded some Scripture Psalm, suitable to it. And these Psalms being chosen out suitably to the new occasions and new conditions of God's people, and sung by them with new hearts and renewed affections, will ever be found new songs. Words of eternal truth and grace, are ever old (as the Gospel is an eternal Gospel) and ever new, as the commandment of love is a new commandment as well as old. And to the new creature all things are made new. Daily mercies are to him new mercies. Duties of humiliation, which have been of ancient practice in the Church, are to him, as new wine. But to an old and carnal heart that lies under the state of vanity and corruption of nature, there is nothing new, no new thing under the sun.

Answer 2: My second answer is that David's exhortation to sing a new song pertained to them in the Old Testament, as well as to us in the New Testament. And yet on new occasions they sang the old songs of David, and that, with acceptance.

Answer 3: My third answer is that Asaph, Haman, and Ethan, were men endued with an infallible measure of a spirit of prophecy, in reciting those Psalms, which the Church of Israel received from them. Give us the like men with the like gifts, and we will receive and sing their Psalms, as the Church of Israel did the other.

Answer 4: My fourth answer is that the places objected out of the revelation, admit a further answer, though the former might serve, the new song mentioned in Revelation 5:9-10 may either be understood metonymically for a doxology or thanksgiving, which the Saints in the Church should give to Christ on occasion to his revealing a clear exposition of the revelation, or else, if it is understood literally, that they sang that very song, as it is there penned by the Holy Spirit, then it appears that at such a time, that song will be translated into number and meter, fit to be sung, and will be sung by the Church, when they will see such a clear exposition of the revelation come to light, as will provoke them to give glory to Christ, who has received power to open the book, and by the same power has redeemed his people, and called them to be kings and priests to God his Father. And so, this place only shows that it will be lawful to sing other songs, besides those of David and Asaph. But yet such only, as are penned by an infallible spirit, or else on occasion, by men of spiritual gifts, which we do not envy.

The song of the 144,000 followers of the Lamb is not expressly said to be a new song, but as it were a new song (Revelation 14:3). New to them who had been accustomed to hear the worshippers of the beast to sing and rejoice in their merits, and superstitious devotions. And new also in respect of the renewed affections, by which they sang it. But yet the same ancient song is sung which talks about the blessed the sheep and saints of Christ, his people, and of their own blessedness in him not imputing their sins to them. So David's Psalms in the spiritual use and sense of them are *new* songs, or as it were new songs to this day, to all that are renewed by grace, to look for their righteousness in Christ, and not in the

Chapter 5: Clearing Objections

works of the Law, of which David was accustomed to sing, no flesh living could be justified by them. And although it was said that no man could learn that song except for the 144,000 who were redeemed from the earth, yet it is not meant of the words and sentences of the song, but of the spiritual sense and use of the song, which no man indeed can learn, but they that have felt the grace and power of their redemption by the Lord Jesus, as no man knows the new name, but they that have received it, (Revelation 2:17).

The song of those who had gotten victory over the beast (Rev. 15) is said to be the song of Moses and of the Lamb. And surely the matter of Moses's song (Exod. 15) might justly yield fit matter for the same doxology on the like occasion; as the same fell out in the 88th year; Rome being spiritual Egypt (Rev. 11:8). And the Pope with his prelates resembling Pharaoh with his taskmasters, and the Spanish Armada marching forth with the like pride and fury, to bring us back to the Egyptian bondage and the redemption from them all being like miraculous, upon which miraculous deliverance, not only the matter of Moses' song, but the very words were also then fitly used, and still may be for a spiritual song of thanksgiving to the Lord, both for that and the same deliverances.

And as for the song of the Lamb, which those that had victory over the beast sang, surely all those songs of David, which celebrate either his own deliverances from Saul, or the deliverance of the Church from Egypt, Babylon, or other enemies, may justly own and bear that title. For when David acknowledges and professes that in his songs, the Spirit of the Lord spoke by him, and that his word was in his tongue. What Spirit of the Lord was that, but the Spirit of the Lord Jesus? And what are then such songs, but the songs of the Lamb, through whose redemption the Church and Saints enjoy all their deliverances? And surely, the song of the Lamb, recorded seems evidently to point at sundry Psalms of David, out of which it was compiled and collected, and which therefore were suitable and fit to be sung on occasion of their victory over the beast, especially with respect and reference to those special sentences, which were fetched from there, though with some small variation, such as is accustomed to be found in all the Scriptures of the New Testament, quoted out of the old.

Revelation 15:3	Psalm 86:10
"Great and marvelous are thy works, Lord God Almighty.	"Thou art great, and dost wondrous things, thou art God alone." "Among the Gods, there is none like unto thee, nor any works like thy works,"

Chapter 5: Clearing Objections

"Just and true are thy ways, thou king of Saints." "Thou only art holy. Who shall not fear thee, O Lord, and glorify thy Name? For all nations shall come and worship before thee. For thy judgments are made manifest," (verse 4).	(Psalm 86:8). "The works of the Lord are great," (Psalm 111:2). "And wonderful," (verse 4). "The works of his hand are truth and judgment," (verse 7). "O thou Holy One of Israel," (Psalm 71:22). "All nations who thou hast made, shall come and worship before thee, O Lord, and glorify thy Name," (Psalm 86:9). "The Lord is known by the judgment which he executeth," (Psalm 9:16). "All men shall fear and shall declare the work of God, for they shall wisely consider of his doings," (Psalm 64:9).

In as much therefore as these who got the victory over the beast, are said to have sang the song of the lamb, and this song of the Lamb is expressly fetched from several words of praise to the Lamb, in several Psalms of David, one of these two things will from here justly be deduced.

1. Either this, that any of those Psalms of David may be sung to the praise of the Lamb, out of which those words of praise are fetched (as when the people of God are said to have praised God with such a word in a Psalm, it is meant they sung the whole Psalm; as, 2 Chron. 5:13; 20, 21; Ezra 3:11) all of them pointing at Psalm 136.

2. That it may be lawful on special and extraordinarily occasions, to compile a spiritual song out of David's words of praise dispersed in several Psalms of David, and other Psalmists in Scripture, and to sing them, composed together as a Psalm of praise to the Lord. And both of these we willingly admit. For these are still the divine meditations, and spiritual expressions of the holy men of God in Scripture, which God has prepared for the setting forth of his own glory.

Objection 7: As the apostle writing to Timothy about prayer in general, and prescribing no form of prayer, it is therefore justly argued, that we are to use no set forms of prayer at all. So the same apostle exhorting the Churches to sing, and not prescribing any form of Psalms, hence I follow, that he does not allow the singing of David's Psalm's. And whatsoever Arguments, strike against stinted forms of prayer, strike against all forms of Prayer as well, as stinting and quenching the Spirit.

Chapter 5: Clearing Objections

Answer 1: My first answer to this is that it is not true that the apostle exhorting to sing, does not prescribe any form of Psalms. For in the same texts where he does exhort the Churches and people of God to sing, he does direct them also to sing *psalms and hymns and spiritual songs.* Which are the express titles of the very forms of the Psalms endited by David and Asaph, as has been showen above? Neither can it be truly said, that he does not allow the singing of David's Psalms. Unless it might be truly said, the Psalms of David are neither psalms, hymns, nor spiritual songs.

Answer 2: My second answer is that the Scriptures put a manifested difference between these two set forms of prayer, and set forms of psalms, also between set forms devised and prescribed by men, and set forms appointed by God; set forms of prayer which the Lord ordinarily prescribed to his people in the Old Testament, or in the New. But set forms of psalms no man doubts, were ordinarily prescribed in the Old Testament, and we suppose in the New Testament also, in the texts alleged.

Again, set forms devised and appointed by men, I will not deny to be justly ejected by the true meaning of the second commandment. But that God forbade us to make to ourselves any images or imaginations and inventions for worship, never forbade himself to devise and appoint for us what form of worship pleased him, either in the Old Testament, or in the New. And therefore whatever arguments strike against set forms of prayer invented and prescribed by men, there is none of them that strike against set forms of Psalms appointed by God. Neither can it with any color be pretended, that the Psalms of David being devised and appointed by the Holy Spirit himself, should either stint or quench the Spirit, unless it might be thought that God's own ordinance to convey and quicken, and enlarge the Spirit should become an impediment and restraint to the Spirit.

Objection 8: The edification of the Church and body of Christ under the New Testament ought to be carried on by the person with all proper gifts of God's Spirit. (Ephesians 4:7-8, 11, 16. 1 Peter 4:10-11. Romans 12:4, 6. 1 Corinthians 12). But in singing of the Psalms of David, there is no more personal gift manifested, and then there is in reading a stinted form of Prayer.

Answer 1: These scriptures prove that God has given the gifts of the Spirit for the edification of his church. And that they who have received the gifts of the spirit, should employ them to the edification of the Church. And some of those Scriptures prove also, that they who have received any gifts, though outward gifts of wealth and honor, should improve and employ them to the good of the Church and should be carried on by the personal and proper gifts of the present members of the Church. For then the Church should not be edified now in these days by the gifts of the penmen of the Scripture, whether Apostles, Prophets, or Evangelists which is expressly repugnant to some of the Scriptures alleged by you. For in Ephesians 4:8 and in 1 Corinthians 12 it is expressly said that "God gave the Apostles, Prophets, and Evangelists, for the edifying of the Church, until the whole body of Christ is perfected at the day of his coming." And lest you should dream of new Apostles to be raised up in every age, the Holy Spirit tells us that the Church of the Jews at their last conversion will be built on the foundation of the Lambs' twelve Apostles. The twelve Apostles of the Lamb will have a fundamental influence in the rearing and building of the Church of the Jews, not by their resurrection to life again in those days, but by the power of the spirit breathing in their gifts and writings. And as Abel being dead yet speaks, and to that edification, so the Apostles though dead also speak, and David being dead speaks, and sings likewise to the edification of the body of Christ, until we come to sing hallelujahs in heavenly glory.

Do not say these writings of the Apostles and Evangelists, of David and the Prophets, do not speak to the edification to the Church, but they are expounded and applied by the spiritual gifts of the ministers and people of God in each age. For the very reading of them is an ordinance of God, and no ordinance of God is empty and beggarly, and destitute of the Spirit. Which is the vanity of men's traditions, and may not be imputed to any of God's ordinances.

"Neither ought you to say, that in singing the Psalms of David, there is no more personal gift manifested, then there is in reading a stinted form of prayer."

For first, in reading a stinted form of prayer, there is no gift of the Spirit at all manifested, but rather as I conceive it, a manifest breach of the second commandment of God, which is a grieving of the Spirit. But in singing of the Psalms of David, there is a gift of the spirit manifested, even the gift of obedience to the command of the Apostle. And that is the personal gift that sings.

Secondly, all the treasures of the gifts of the Spirit breathing in the Psalms of David are likewise manifested in the reverent and holy singing of them. You might more truly have said, there is no more personal gift of the Spirit manifested in singing the Psalms of David, then in reading the Psalms of David, because either of both those duties are alike acts of obedience to God's Commandment. But if you had so said, your objection had answered itself.

Objection 9: Many of God's people now have gifts to compose spiritual songs, as well as carnal poets to make carnal sonnets, or as drunkards that make songs of God's people. Now everyone that has a gift is to administer it by

Chapter 5: Clearing Objections

Christ's Command. And if any for want of experience of such a gift is to administer it by Christ's Command. And if any for want of experience of such a gift in themselves, should question it, they may consider the promise of powering out the Spirit in a more plentiful measure, now in the days of the New Testament, then in the old.

Answer 1: To this, my first answer is that, although many of God's people have gifts to compose spiritual songs, as well as carnal poets' carnal sonnets, and drunkards' profane sonnets, yet that will not argue, that the spiritual songs, which of God's people have gifts to compose, are fit to be sung in the public holy assemblies of the saints, no more than the carnal and profane sonnets of drunken poets are fit to be sung in civil assemblies. Let drunken carnal poets sing their carnal sonnets in their taverns and alehouses, and such of God's people as have received a gift to compose a spiritual song fit for their private solace, sing it in their private houses. But every spiritual song, fit for private solace, is not fit to be sung in the solemn assemblies of the Church for public edification. No more than it is fit for every private Christian who has a gift to compose a spiritual prayer, to utter and power forth the same in the public congregation of the Church.

Answer 2: My second answer is that it is more probable then, that many of the people of God in the Old Testament had gifts to compose spiritual songs aside from David and

Asaph, and yet unless their gift was carried along by an infallible Spirit, they were not received among the songs of the temple.

Answer 3: My third answer is this. Suppose that spiritual songs composed by an ordinary gift might be received among the public songs of the congregation, yet will it there follow, that the Church will be bound to sing only such songs, and deprive themselves of psalms, hymns, and spiritual songs of David and Asaph, which were composed with a far larger measure and power of the Holy Spirits?

Answer 4: My fourth answer is that it is readily granted that as every man has received a gift, so let him administer and dispense it, according to the text alleged. But yet in Christ's way, every private gift is not fit for public administration, and neither is every public gift fit to be administrated to the shouldering out of a greater gift then itself.

Answer 5: My fifth answer is that if such as lack the experience of such a gift of spiritual poetry in themselves, should be encouraged to expect it from the promise of powering out the Spirit *on all flesh* in the days of the Gospel, (Acts 2:17) they might as well look for the gifts of tongues, healing, and miracles. For it is the same Spirit which is promised to be powered out upon all flesh. Let every man

Chapter 5: Clearing Objections

administer the gifts of the Spirit, according to the measure which he has received within his own life.

Objection 10: But as the Lord is as full of the Spirit now to help us to indict Psalms, as in the days of David and Asaph. And it seems a dishonor to Christ, to dispense his word by reading and singing, without the exercise of the glorious and various administrations of the spiritual gifts of the New Testament.

Answer 1: The Lord is as full of the Spirit now, and as able to furnish us with a prophetical spirit now to indict prophetical Scriptures, as he did furnish the Prophets in the Old Testament. But yet God thought it no dishonor to Christ to leave us the Scriptures of the old Prophets for our edification in the New Testament, as well as in the Old. It is the same Spirit of the same Christ that spoke by the Prophets of the Old Testament, and speaks in the saints of the New. And it is no dishonor to Christ to dispense his word, and to guide the body of his Church, as well by the unity of the same Spirit, as by the variety of the diverse' gifts of the Spirit now. And although we do not exercise the glorious and various administrations of the spiritual gifts of the New Testament, in the indicting of new Psalms, no more than in the indicting of new Scriptures. Yet we can neither sing the old Psalms of David, nor read the old Scriptures of the Prophets acceptably to God, nor comfortably to ourselves without the exercise of the gracious and various spiritual gifts of the New Testament.

Objection 11: We have examples in the New Testament, of exercising personal gifts, as well in singing, as in praying and prophesying, which Epistle is directed to all the saints in all places. And consequently, that Church is to be precedential in dispensing personal gifts in this ordinance of singing, as well as in any other.

Answer 1: My first answer is that the direction given in that Epistle to the Church of Corinth, we willingly grant are precedential to all the Churches, as well as the directions given in other Epistles to other Churches. And the directions there given in dispensing spiritual gifts, prophecy is preferred before tongues, nor any tongues dispensed without interpretation, that order is observed without confusion, that diverse people may speak without interruption, that no man may speak without subjection, that women are not permitted to speak to usurpation, that all things are done to edification. And all of these directions are precedential to all such Churches as have received the like gifts. But there is no direction given to the Church of Corinth, or any other, that every man should have a gift of tongues, or a gift of compiling a Psalm, or if he has a gift of compiling a Psalm for his private use by an ordinary spirit, then he should present it to be sung beore the whole Church, and the Church to say amen to his

Chapter 5: Clearing Objections

Psalm. For the gift of Psalms, which the Apostle there speaks of, was not an ordinary gift to compile some spiritual ditty in the verse, but extraordinary, as joined with the gift of strange tongues, for it appears by the context, that the gift of tongues was used by the members of the Church of Corinth in four ways. 1. In speaking mysteries (verse two), 2. In prayer (verse 14), 3. In singing (verse 15), and 4. In thanksgiving (verse 17)." So that the singing there mentioned, was by an extraordinary gift, as the tongues were, in which it was dispensed.

Objection 12: Indeed the gift of tongues, in which these Psalms seem to be uttered was extraordinary, but it does not follow that the gift of composing those Psalms were extraordinary gifts, no more than prayer, where when it was joined, or prophecy. Singing psalms and prophecy does not otherwise differ than poetry and prose. And if it was extraordinary in the Corinthians, we do not have warrant for public ordinary singing in the New Testament from an example.

Answer 1: As the gift of tongues was extraordinary, so was every ordinance dispensed in it, whether prayer, singing psalms, or prophecy, all of them extraordinary, both for sublimity of matter (in the Spirit he speaks mysteries in verse 2) and for power and demonstration of the Spirit, and for suddenness and dexterity of utterance without previous study, or meditation, as Acts 2:4, 11. Though there is an ordinary gift of prayer and prophesying, as well as of singing? Yet nevertheless, the apostles and prophets had an extraordinary gift of prayer and prophesying. And so had those Corinthians also an extraordinary gift (although in less measure) of praying and prophesying and singing also.

It is not credible that he who would have new wine put into new bottles, would power forth ordinary and common matters in new tongues, and so raise extraordinary expectation of ordinary things.

Answer 2: It is an uncouth comparison, to make no more difference between singing psalms and prophecy, then between poetry and prose. In prophecy we open the Scriptures and counsels of God. In Psalms we open the counsels and thanksgivings of our own hearts, in psalms we sing to glorify God, in prophecy we speak to edify men. You might with far more reason and congruity have said, *That prayer and singing Psalms differ no otherwise then poetry and prose.* And yet there is more difference even between them, as the Apostle James notes. (James 5:13).

Answer 3: When you say, that if the singing in the Church of Corinth was extraordinary, then we have no warrant for our public ordinary singing in the New Testament from any example. Neither does the argument follow, nor if it did, is it of any force. For although this example of singing in the Church of Corinth was extraordinary. Yet that singing of Christ and his disciples at the last supper was ordinary (Matthew 26:30). And although there were no examples of public ordinary singing in the New Testament, yet it is enough that there is a precept of public ordinary singing to the Churches, both of the Ephesians and the Colossians. And what the Spirit speaks to those Churches, it speaks to all.

CHAPTER 6:

Propounding a second and third argument, for the singing of David's Psalms.

Having cleared the first argument, for the singing of David's Psalms, and such like scripture psalms, let us now proceed to a second argument, taken from the end and use of the Psalms of David. The Psalms of David and Asaph and the like, were written for a threefold end, as we see expressed by the Apostle in Colossians 3:16. In other words, 1. For instruction, or teaching. 2. For admonition. 3. For singing praise to the Lord.

Now, if the Psalms of David and the same were written (doubtlessly they were) in the Old Testament for this threefold end, and each of them moral (that is, of general and perpetual use) and none of them are abrogated in the New Testament, then it would be a sacrilegious sin to take away from the Psalms either of the two former uses (the use of instruction, or admonition), so it will be alike sacrilege to deprive them of the threefold use, by forbidding them to be sung for praise and thanksgiving to the Lord. Where, to a third argument may be added, *taken from the duty of singing psalms every Sabbath*. And the defect of provision of other Psalms if the Psalms of David, and other Scripture Psalms are refused. It appears from Psalm 95:1-2, 7 that "when we present ourselves

Chapter 6: Singing David's Psalms

before the Lord, to hear the voice of his word, we should come before his presence with singing of Psalms." If so, then some must have a gift, either to prepare set forms of Psalms beforehand for every Sabbath day, or at least a gift, upon the present occasion, suddenly to invent and utter a Psalm fit for the present Sabbath from week to week. Neither of both which are easy to be believed. For if it were so, then doubtlessly Christ would have appointed some or other officer to attend to this duty of compiling psalms, as he has appointed elders to attend to the ministry of the word, and prayers. Or else we would inspire some or other member of the Church with such a gift and spirit of palmistry as might suit the occasions of the Church from Sabbath to Sabbath. But neither of both these do we find, either in the Scriptures of the New Testament, or in experience, we find neither ordinance appointing it, or providence granting it. And yet it is evident that the gracious providence of God, is not lacking in supplying well-ordered Churches, with all such gifts of preaching and prayer, and rule, and the like, as God has required for the edification of the Church to the end of the world. Neither is it credible that Christ would take us off from singing the Psalms of David and Asaph, which were of divine and infallible inspiration, and leave us to an uncertain and common gifts of private brethren.

It is said that the Church of Corinth lacked no such gifts of Psalms, nor such members as did compile in 1 Corinthians 14:26.

That is true, and neither did they want the gift of tongues and of revelation in the same text. But there were extraordinary gifts, fit to glorify Christ in his first ascension into glory, and fit to commend and confirm the Gospel to pagans, but nowhere promised to be continued to Churches in after ages, nor nowhere commanded to be imitated. Much less our common gifts, and the Psalms indicted by the same to be substituted in their rooms, and David's Psalms to be silenced, that our Psalms might be attended.

CHAPTER 7:

Concerning the singers.

And first, whether one above to sing, or the whole Church.

The third question about singing of Psalms, concerns the singers. For although vocal singing is approved, and also the singing of David's Psalms, yet still it remains to some a question, who must sing them? Here a threefold scruple arises again. One, whether one is to sing for all the rest, and the rest joining only in spirit, and saying amen? Two, whether women, as well as man, or only men? Three, whether carnal men and pagans may be permitted to sing with us or Christians alone, and Church Members?

Touching the first of these scruples, it is without a doubt that a Christian man for his own private solace and edification may sing a Psalm alone by himself, as Asaph had his songs by night (Psalm 77:6). 2. It is granted, that he who had a spiritual and extraordinary gift of indicting a Psalm, might sing it himself and the rest of the Church join with him in spirit, saying *amen*. Though in the Old Testament, he that indicted the Psalm, gave it to the masters of song, to be sung publicly, by others as well as himself. But the question is of singing the Psalms of David and other Scripture Psalms, whether they are to be sung by the whole congregation, or by one alone for all the rest, saying amen. And to make good this way.

Objection 1: It is alleged, in the Church of Corinth, one had a Psalm (1 Corinthians 14:26). And he that had a Psalm sung in the Spirit, and was directed to sing with understanding also, that they might join with him in Spirit and say *amen* (verses 15-16).

My answer to this is that, this only concerned the extraordinary Psalms, indicted by such as had also a gift of tongues as well as of Psalms. For therefore, it is by a spiritual gift to sing with understanding also, in other words, with the understanding of the Church. But this does not concern the singing of the Psalms of David, which are now not given by any peculiar gift to any single man.

Objection 2: It is also alleged that singing of Psalms is an act of Prophecy. And that the prophets were to speak one after another, and if anything were revealed to another that sat by, the first was to hold his peace.

Answer 1: Prophecy is taken two ways in the Scripture, to omit other acceptations of the Word, not pertinent to the point in hand. 1. Sometimes more strictly and properly, for preaching, that is, for expounding and applying Scripture to edification. 2. Sometimes more largely, for the publishing of spiritual things to the glory of God, and edification of

Chapter 7: Should the Whole Church Sing?

ourselves or others. And in this sense, Master Perkins makes two parts of it: preaching of the word, and prayer. Which he quotes, "Abraham is a Prophet, and he shall pray for thee," (Genesis 20:7). He also quotes that where the sons of Asaph, Hama, and Jeduthun, who were singers, are said to prophecy with harps (1 Chron. 25:1). Which argues that singing of Psalms as well as prayer, may in some sense be called an act of Prophecy. But in this sense Paul does not speak of prophecy, for he does expressly distinguish it from prayer, and much more from singing (1 Cor. 11:4-5). And in 1 Corinthians 14, he plainly distinguishes prophecy from singing of Psalms, for when he exhorts them to covet after spiritual gifts, chiefly, that they might prophecy, (verse 1), it is not his meaning that they should chiefly covet after the gift of indicting or singing Psalms, but rather after the gift of preaching, in other words, of expounding and applying Scripture to edification. When therefore, Paul directed the Prophets to speak one by one (verses 30-31), he does not speak of that kind of prophecy where many may sing one and the same Psalms together, but the other kind of prophecy, which is preaching. How is it true also, that if many will sing several Psalms at once and the same time together in one and the same congregation, it would breed the like confusion in the church, as if the Prophets should speak two or three, or more of them at once.

It is said, *Why is it not a conclusion for so many voices to join together in singing a Psalm, though it be one and the same Psalm?*

Answer: No more now in the New Testament, then it was in the old, when the trumpeters and singers were as one, to make one found to be heard in praising the Lord. "And when they lift up their voice, with the trumpeters, and cymbals, and instruments of music, and praised the Lord, saying, for he is good, and his mercy undereth forever," (2 Chronicle 5:13). For then God showed his approbation and acceptance of them, and of their worship. And surely, if the concourse and consent of so many voices had been a confusion, doubtless it would have been as much displeasing to God in the old testament, as in the New. For God is not a God of confusion in the Churches of the Saints, whether the New Testament, or in the Old. And if our desire is that the Will of God may be done on Earth as it is done by the Angels in Heaven, we read of a "multitude of an heavenly host of Angels, praising God, and saying, Glory be to God on High, *etc.*" (1 Corinthians 14:33), without any confusion.

Objection 3: Very little example can be given of any entire congregation that snag together, mentioned in Scripture.

Although no example could be given, yet it is a sufficient warrant for the Duty, if any precept has been given

Chapter 7: Should the Whole Church Sing?

of it in Scripture, and the precept is plain in Colossians 3:16, where the whole Church of Colossi is exhorted to have "the word of Christ dwell richly in them," not only to teach and admonish one another, but also to sing the Psalms with holy melody to the Lord. If God had reserved this duty to some select choristers, he would have given some direction in the New Testament for their qualification and election. But since he does not speak of any such select musicians, he commands this duty *to the whole Church.*

Answer 2: It is not safely said that scarce any example in the Scripture can be given of any entire congregation that sang together.

For, 1. in Exodus 15:1, Moses and the Children of Israel are said to have sung a song of thanksgiving to the Lord. And the same, they, that sang this song, are the same soon to forget God's works, and not wait for his counsel, but to fall lusting (Psalm 106:12-14) which was the body of the people.

2. Christ and his Disciples, when they administrated and received the Lord's Supper, they were an entire congregation. "And after the supper sung a Psalm or Hymn," (Matthew 26:30). To say, that one sang it, and the other joined in spirit, saying *amen*, has no foothold in the text. It might as well be said that they *all* took the bread, *all* blessed it, broke it, gave it, in that one did it and all the rest joined in

Spirit, and consented, and like enough to the blessing of it, said *amen*.

3. It is no strain of the mind, but a solid and judicious exposition of the fourth chapter of the Revelation, to make it a description of a particular visible Church of Christ, according to the platform and pattern of the New Testament. Where, as the four living creatures, are the four sorts of officers, to the twenty-four Elders that set forth the brethren of the Church, who are as Elders (in respect of their ripe age, (Galatians 4:1-3) and twenty four in number answering to the twenty four orders of priests and Levites (1 Chronicle 25:9). And all these are said to join together in "singing a new song unto the Lamb," (Revelation 5:8-10).

Objection 4: If the whole Church should sing together, then all the members were teachers. For the Apostle bids us to teach and admonish one another in Psalms (Colossians 3:16). But the same Apostle denies all them to be teachers, (1 Corinthians 12:29).

Answer 1: Although the Apostle bids us to teach and admonish one another in Psalms, yet he does not say, that we should teach one another by singing Psalms together, but he there holds forth a twofold use and improvement of the whole word of God dwelling richly in us, and a threefold use and improvement of the Psalms. The whole word of God dwelling richly in us is to be improved to the teaching and admonishing of one another. But the Psalms are to be improved, not only to both of these ends (as all the rest of the World beside) but to a third end also, even to the singing of praises to the Lord. Now in this third end, the entire congregation may join in improving the Psalms to them, although not in public teaching or admonishing of the Church by them, yet in setting forth the praises, the counsels, the works of God declared to them.

Answer 2: Also, though not everyone who sings a Psalm may be fit to teach or admonish them that sing with him, yet he that appoints the Psalm to be sung, may be said to teach and admonish the whole congregation that are to sing it, or hear it. Julian the Apostate, took himself to be admonished, and indeed reproved the Christians when they sang in his hearing the 115th and 97th Psalms, which declared the vanity of idols, and the confusion of such as worship them, as is recorded in the Church Story by Socrates, Theodore, and Nicephorus.

Answer 3: Also, although the Apostle denies that everyone should be a teacher, his meaning is only to deny, that they are all teachers by public office, to attend upon expounding and applying Scripture to public edification. But it was not part of his meaning to forbid private teaching, or admonishing one another (for then, Aquila and Priscilla had gone too far in instructing Apollos in Acts 18:26), or to forbid the quickening and edifying of the Spirit of one another, by singing together Psalms of instruction, admonition, consolation to themselves, and prayers and praises to the Lord.

CHAPTER 8:

Whether women may sing as well as men.

The second scruple about singers is whether women may be allowed to sing as well as men. In this point there are some that deal with us, as Pharaoh dealt with the Israelites, who though he was at first utterly unwilling that any of them should go to sacrifice to the Lord in the wilderness, yet being at length convinced that they must go, then he was content the men should go, but not the women (Exodus 10:11). So here, some that were altogether against singing Psalms at all with a lively voice, yet being convinced that it is a moral worship of God warranted in Scripture, then if there must be singing, one alone must sing, or if all, the men only, and not the women.

Objection 1: And their reason is because it is not permitted for a woman to speak in Church in 1 Corinthians 14:34. How then will they sing? Also, much less is it permitted to them to prophecy in the Church (1 Timothy 2:11-12) and singing Psalms is a kind of prophesying.

Answer 1: One answer will remove both of these scruples, and withal declare the truth. It is apparent by the scope and context of both of those Scriptures that a woman is not permitted to speak in the Church, in two ways.

1. By teaching, whether in expounding, or applying Scripture. For this, the Apostle accounts an act of authority,

which is unlawful for a woman to usurp over the man (1 Timothy 2:12). And besides, the woman is more subject to error then the man (verse 14). And therefore might soon prove a seducer if she became a teacher.

2. It is not permitted for a woman to speak in church, by way of propounding questions, though under the pretense and desire to learn for her own satisfaction, but rather it is required that she should ask her husband at home (1 Corinthians 14:35).

For under pretense of questioning for learning's sake, she might so propound her question, as to teach her teachers, or if not so, yet to open a door to some of her own weak and erroneous apprehensions, or at least soon exceed the bounds of womanly modesty.

Nevertheless, in two other cases, it is clear that a woman is allowed to speak in the church in way of subjection, when she is to give account of her offence. Similarly, Peter questioned Sapphira before the Church touching the price of land sold by her and her husband, which her husband had concealed by his lie. And she accordingly spoke in the Church to give an answer to his question in Acts 5:8, in way of singing forth the praises of the Lord, together with the rest of the congregation. For it is evident that the apostle lays no greater restraint on the women for silence in the Church, then the Law had put on them before. For so speaking the place alleged

Chapter 8: Can Women Sing?

he says, "It is not permitted to the women to speak, but to be under subjection, as also saith the Law," (1 Corinthians 14:34). The Apostle then requires the same subjection in the woman, which the Lord had put on them no more. Now, it is certain the Law, indeed the Lawgiver Moses, did permit Miriam and the women that went out after her to sing forth praises of the Lord, as well as the men, and to answer the men in their song of thanksgiving. "Sing ye to the Lord, for he hath triumphed gloriously, the horse and his rider hath he thrown into the sea," (Exodus 20:21). Which may be a ground sufficient to justify me in the lawful practice of women singing together with men the praises of the Lord. And accordingly the ancient practice of women in the primitive Churches to sing the public praises of the Lord, we read recorded in the *Ecclesiastical History of Socrates*, Book 2, and Chapter 18 of the *Greek Gospel* and chapter 16 of the Latin, also in Theodore's *third book*, Chapter 17.

CHAPTER 9:

Whether carnal men may sing, as well as godly Christians?

The third scruple about the singers remains; whether carnal men and pagans may be permitted to sing with us, or Christians alone, and church members?

What we believe in this point may be summed up in these three points.

1. That the Church and the members thereof are called to sing the Praises of God, and to their mutual edification. For, they were Churches of Christ, and members of Churches, whom the apostle exhorts to speak to themselves, and make melody to the Lord with psalms and hymns and spiritual songs. (Ephesians 5:19, Colossians 3:16).

2. That the praising of God with Psalms is comely for the Christians, whether received into the fellowship of any particular visible Church, or not. For so much do the words of David hold forth. "Praise is comely for the upright," (Psalm 33:13).

3. Though spiritual gifts are necessary to make melody to the Lord in singing, yet spiritual gifts are neither the only, nor chief ground of singing, but the chief ground thereof is the moral duty lying upon all men by the commandment of God. "If any be merry to sing Psalms," (James 5:13). As in prayer,

though spiritual gifts are requisite to make it acceptable, yet the duty of prayer lies on all men, by that commandment which forbids Atheism. It is "the fool that saith in his heart, there is no God," of whom it is said, "they call not upon the Lord," (Psalm 14:1, 4). Which also may serve for a just argument and proof of the point.

1. If the commandment of God and indeed by the light of nature, if all men are bound to pray to God in their distress (as even Jonah's mariners will confess in a storm in Jonah 1:6), then all men are likewise bound to sing to the praise of God in their deliverances, and comforts. For the word runs alike level. "Is any afflicted? Let him pray. Is any merry? Let him sing Psalms," (James 5:13).

A second proof may be taken from the general commandment to all men upon the earth to sing to the Lord. "Sing unto the Lord all the earth," (Psalm 100:12). "Make a joyful noise unto the Lord all ye lands, come before his presence with singing," (Psalm 68:32). "Sing unto the Lord all the kingdoms of the Earth, O sing Praises unto the Lord." And indeed the grounds and ends of singing, though some of them do more peculiarly concern the Church and people of God (and therefore they of all others are most bound to abound in this duty), yet sundry of the grounds and ends of singing are common to all the sons of men, and therefore none of them are to be exempted from this service. As the sovereignty of God,

"The Lord is a great God, and a great King above all Gods," (Psalm 95:3). And therefore, "Make a joyful noise to him with Psalms, he is to be feared above all Gods, and therefore sing unto him all the Earth," (Psalm 96:4).

The greatness of God's works of creation and providence, are other grounds of singing, and they concern all the sons of men in common. "The Lord giveth food to all flesh," (Psalm 145:6, 10). Therefore, let all flesh bless his holy name. "Let everything that has breathed praise the Lord for his mighty acts, and for his excellent greatness," (Psalm 150:2, 6). The end of singing is to praise the Lord for his goodness, and to stir up ourselves and others to serve the Lord for his goodness, and to stir up ourselves and others to serve the Lord with cheerfulness and glad hearts. And therefore, travelers, prisoners, sickmen, and seamen, being saved from several distresses by the good hand of God, all of them are commanded to "praise the Lord for his goodness, and to declare his wonders before the sons of men," (Psalm 107:6,32).

Objection 1: Against the singing of all sorts of men in the congregation, carnal as well as Christian, is taken from the examples of song set forth in Scripture, which both in the Old Testament, and in the New, were only performed by the Church and Church-members. As the song of Moses, and the children of Israel in Exodus 15:1. Concerning his other song in Deuteronomy 32, he was commanded to teach it to the

Chapter 9: Can Carnal Men Sing?

children of Israel. The song of Deborah was sung by her and Barak in Judges 5:1. Under the kings of Judah, and after the return from captivity, the officers of the Church only sang for the more orderly carrying on of that ordinance in 1 Chronicles 6:31-32, 16:4. In the New Testament, Christ and his Apostles sang in a place apart from others (Matthew 26:30). In the Church of Corinth, none but the brethren had liberty of prophecy, in teaching or singing Psalms. In the Revelation, the four beasts, and the twenty four elders, and the 144,000 who sang the praises of God and of the Lamb, were apparent representations of the Church, her officers and members.

Answer 1: My first answer is that all these examples prove nothing more but what we willingly grant, and what in the former part of this discourse, we have been occasioned to maintain and prove, in other words, that it is lawful, not only for one man alone, but for a *whole* Church, officers and members, to sing the praises of the Lord in heart and voice together with one accord, and so much in all these places do evince.

Secondly, we do not live by examples only, but by precepts also. And evident precepts have been alleged already, for the general practice of singing by all the sons of men on the face of the earth.

My third answer is, that these examples allow even wicked men and apostates to sing, though it is to upraise and convince their wickedness. As that song of Moses in Deuteronomy 32 was appointed to be sung by the children of Israel, not only in Canaan, but in their state of apostate and calamity. "When evil should befall them in the latter days," (Deuteronomy 31:19-22, 29).

Objection 2: It is one of the peculiar privileges of the Church, that the public dispensation of the Word is committed only to them in Romans 3:2 and 9:4. But singing for the matter of it, is nothing else but the Word. And the act of singing in public is the public dispensation of it.

Answer 1: The public dispensation of the Word, in other words, by preaching, that is, by exposition and application of the word, and that in way of office, is committed only to the Church, and to some select members of the Church, chiefly for the Church's sake, though the benefit of it may redound also to men without. But the public dispensation of the Word is not so confined to the Church, but that occasionally men without may publicly as well as privately, dispense the counsel and will of God both to the Church, and to men out of the Church. And it may be a sin both in God's people and in others, not to hearken to it. Pharaoh Necho, yet his ambassadors, publicly declared the counsel of God to Josiah. And it was a dangerous sin in Josiah, that he did not hearken to the words of Necho, which the text says "were from the mouth of God," (2 Chronicles 35:21-12). Balaam publicly

Chapter 9: Can Carnal Men Sing?

dispensed the counsel and word of God throughout the 23rd and 24th chapters of Numbers, to Balack and the princes of Moab. And it was a desolating sin in Balack and the princes of Moab, that they did not hearken to him. And it would have been a sin in the Church of Israel also, if they hearing of the same, had not received his prophecies (which God put into his mouth) as the word of God. The King of Philistines reproved both Abraham and Sarah from the word of the Lord, (Genesis 20:9-10, 16). And it had been a sin in them both, to have neglected his reproof.

Answer 2: It is one thing publicly to dispense any ordinance or worship of God, which is peculiar to the church, and another thing to join with the Church in such parts of the public worship of God, which are not peculiar for the public prayers and praises of God, and to the Psalms also, which though they are dispensed and offered up in the very words of God, yet due praises are not therefore the more undue, because they are offered up in due words.

Objection 3: It is confusion of the Church and the world to sing together, in a mixed assembly.

Answer 1: All that are out of the Church, are not forthwith the world, many are called out of the world, (and so indeed all ought to be, except the children of the faithful) before they are received into the Church. Though they do sing with the Church, yet it is not a singing of the Church and world together, because they are not of the world, but Christ has called them out of the world, and the world hates them.

Answer 2: It is no confusion, but lawful communion, for the Church and the world to join together in a mixed assembly, to perform such duties, as God requires of them in common. As to hear the word of God, and the like. In Antioch in Pisidia, the whole city almost came to hear the word of God in Acts 13:44. Was this confusion? And what if the Apostles had prayed in that mixed assembly, and all the faithful had said *amen* to their prayers, and what if Pagans also understanding what they prayed, had said amen with them, had it been confusion? Indeed, what if in such an assembly, they should not part without the public praises of God in a Psalm, and that whole mixed assembly should join together in the singing of it, would it be a confusion? If it is of confusion for all sorts of men to join together in a mixed assembly to hear the word of God, because it is a duty required of them all, then neither is it a confusion, but a lawful communion to join together in singing the praises of God in a Psalm, but it is a duty required of them all. David foretells, "That all the Kings of the earth shall praise the Lord, when they hear the words of his mouth. Yea they shall sing in the ways of the Lord, that great is the glory of the Lord," (Psalm 138:45).

Objection 4: The end of singing is to instruct, admonish, and comfort the Church. But the world must not instruct the Church, the Church having received sufficient gifts by Christ's ascension to edify itself (Ephesians 4:7-12). This was to borrow jewels of the Egyptians to make a golden calf, to put the Ark into a cart to be drawn by oxen that should be carried by Levites.

Answer 1: To this my first answer is that the end of singing is not only to instruct, admonish, and comfort the Church, but also those godly, throughout the Church. Praise is good for the upright, whether in the Church or out of it. Furthermore, the end of singing is not only to instruct, and admonish and comfort the upright, but also to instruct, and convince, and reprove the wicked as has been shown in Deuteronomy 31:19.

Answer 2: My second answer that the end of singing, is not only to instruct, and convince and edify men, but also to praise and glorify God in singing Psalm 96:1-2. Although the Church may be sufficient to edify itself, it is not yet sufficient to glorify God alone, which is a duty lying on all the sons of men, indeed in their kind, upon all the creatures.

Answer 3: Thirdly, although the Church has received from Christ's ascension sufficient helps within itself, to edify itself. Yet if his providence also casts in other helps from without to edify it, it is from the virtue of the same ascension of Christ sitting at God's right hand, and such helps are not to be rejected. Josiah did not do well to reject the admonition of Pharaoh Neco. Abraham and Sarah did well to receive the admonition of Abimelech. And yet neither Pharaoh nor Abimelech were of the Church.

Answer 4: My fourth answer is that the admonition and instruction given in the singing of a Psalm, is rather given by him that penned the Psalm, and by him that appoints the Psalm to be sung, then by every singer, unless the admonition and instruction are to himself by the words. And unless there is a stirring up of affection to himself and others, by the blessing of God on the harmony.

Answer 5: My fifth answer is that, although it was an abuse of the Egyptian Jewels, to borrow them to make a golden calf, yet it was no abuse of them to offer them to God for the building and furnishing of the work of the Tabernacle. God forbid any Christian soul should please itself in comparing the praises of the holy and glorious God to the golden calf, for although the singing of the praises of God by carnal men may be compared to the employment of the Egyptian Jewels to that end for which they are used. Yet that end being the praising of God and in such a way as God has enjoyed to all men, it is not an employment of Egyptian Jewels to the making of a golden calf, but to the praises of the living

Chapter 9: Can Carnal Men Sing?

God, who is the Savior of all men, especially of all them that believe.

Neither is there any resemblance between putting the ark on a cart to be carried by oxen, which should have been carried by Levites, and the permitting of men out of the Church to join in singing the praises of the Lord. For neither do the members of the Church lay aside this duty, and leave it to non-Members, neither are non-Members as a cart and oxen, upon whom this duty was never laid. But all of them are enjoined, as to hear his word, and to call on his name, and to sing forth the praises due to his name from all of his creatures. There is much more just cause of fear, lest this new opinion of rejecting of singing of David's Psalms, and disallowing any Psalms to be sung, but such as are invented by ordinary common gifts, and the same to be sung only be them that invent them, lest this new opinion, I say, be *worse* than the new cart of the Philistines, for that was to carry the ark of God to his place, but this new opinion tends to carry this ordinance of singing Psalms out of the country. And there is the same cause of fear lest over prizing our personal spiritual common gifts, and the Psalms indicted by them, above the Psalms of David, are not indeed the erecting of a golden calf, instead of the Cherubim of the Tabernacles.

Objection 5: But if Pagans and profane people may sing, they may also prophecy in Christ's Spiritual Temple.

It is been shown above that prophecy is taken two ways in Scripture. More properly for teaching the Word, that is, expounding and applying Scripture to edification. More generally for speaking or publishing the holy things of God, to the *glory of God*. In the former of these ways, it is not for Pagans or the profane, ordinarily and allowably to Prophecy in Christ's Spiritual Temple, which is His Church. But in the latter way, it is not unlawful as to say amen, to the public prayers of the Church, and thereby to express their joining in prayer, so to join with them in singing Psalms, which it has been shown above, is a duty common to them within the Church, as well as to join with them in hearing the Word. In which, whether they edify the Church or not, certainly it tends to the glory of God, that God's praises should be set forth by all the sons of men. And it is a further glory to God, that such pagans and profane people should sing the Word of God to their own conviction and confusion of face; and from both, some edification and comfort redounds to the Church, to see the wicked convinced, and God's Name to be glorified. For it is an honor to God, and a comfort to His Church, that our God is not as *their* God, our enemies being judges and witnesses.

Objection 6: The godly Jews would not suffer the Samaritans to build the Temple with them although they offered themselves (Ezra 4:2-3). And if singing is prophesying

Chapter 9: Can Carnal Men Sing?

in any sense, and any way tending to the comfort or edification of the Church, why should we suffer profane people to sing with us?

Answer 1: That the godly Jews rejected the Samaritans from building with them, it was not out of moral consideration, as if it were unlawful for heathens to contribute their assistance to the worship or ordinances of God, but out of a ceremonial respect, because no heathens or unclean people might be allowed to come into the Temple of the Lord. (Acts 21:26 and 2 Chronicles 23:19). But by the death of Christ the partition wall of ceremonies is broken down. And we may allow heathens and profane people to come into our holy assemblies in 1 Chronicles 14:24, which they would not admit. Certainly it is the godly Jews themselves who received liberal contributions and oblations from the Kings of Persia, towards the building and maintenance of the Temple in Ezra 7:21-24 and 8:24-30, which was a moral acknowledgement of the honor due to the God of Israel, as well as by Gentiles as Jews. If therefore, the Jews would accept acknowledgement of moral homage and service from heathens and profane men, people given over to the God of Israel, why may not Christians accept from pagans and profane people, their acknowledgement of moral homage and service to our God, in singing forth his praises among us?

Objection 7: But such carnal and profane people are not worthy to take the Name and Praises of God into their mouths, nor are they able to make melody to the Lord, by singing to him with grace in their hearts, as is required in Colossians 3:16.

Answer 1: Firstly, if we speak of the worthiness of desert, John the Baptist was not worthy to loose the latchet of Christ's shoe, much less to sing forth his glorious praise but if we speak of the worthiness of fitness, though it is true, their unclean lips are not fit to take the holy word of God into their mouths, yet the holy word of God is fit to come into their minds and mouths also, to convince and reprove them of their apostate from God, and rebellion against him in Deuteronomy 31:19. And however they are unfit and unworthy to take God's Name and praise into their mouths, yet surely the Lord is worthy of all praise and glory, blessing and thanksgiving from them, and all the creatures which he has made.

Answer 2: Secondly, it is true, carnal and profane people are not able to make melody, and sing to the Lord with grace in their hearts, yet that defect does not more excuse carnal people from singing, then it excuses them from prayer, which they cannot perform acceptably to God, without a spirit of grace and faith. To pray and so to sing, without faith is a sin, but not to pray at all is a greater sin. The one is a hypocrite, the other is atheist.

Chapter 9: Can Carnal Men Sing?

Objection 8: Although the Scribes and Pharisees joined in the temple songs on the words of David in the worldly Sanctuary, yet the melody made by such carnal and clean mouths, were far more beautiful and glorious, then ours in the assemblies made, with a multitude of all manner of singers, upon the same words of David and Asaph. For although they that sang in the Temple in those days were carnal, yet they were appointed to sing, and were choice singers, endued with choice singing gifts, which made the service most beautiful, as men call beauty. But the melody of our assembly compared with theirs, has no outward beauty in it. So that if their melody were a type of ours, then the type is more glorious then the antitype, which is a dishonor to Christ.

Answer 1: Actually, it is no dishonor at all to Christ that the type should be far more beautiful and glorious to the outward man then the antitype. Solomon was a type of Christ, and the Temple of Solomon was a type of his body, and both Solomon himself and his temple were far more beautiful and glorious then Christ himself to the outward man, (Isaiah 53:2). Yet this was no dishonor to Christ, whose beauty and glory was so divine and heavenly in the inner man, that all their outward beauty and glory, were only dim and dark shadows to it.

Answer 2: We do not say that their melody in the temple, which was made with voices, was a type of our melody made with our voices, and singing the same Psalms of David and Asaph. For although their choristers were *types* of the whole Church and their instruments of music were *types* of the inward affections of our hearts, in singing forth the praises of the Lord, to the honor of his name, and to their own edification.

Answer 3: Although their melody might be more beautiful and glorious to the outward appearance, as being more artificial and more musical. Yet seeing the spirit of grace is more abundantly poured out in the New Testament, then in the Old, if the holy singers sing with more life and grace of the Spirit, our melody is the more beautiful and glorious before the Lord, and his spiritual Saints, although theirs were more beautiful and glorious in the outward sense.

Answer 4: Finally. Whether any of the Scribes and Pharisees were musicians of the Temple, endued with choice gifts, and appointed to that office, although we do not know it, yet neither will we deny it. But this we daresay, that if they were appointed to sing, so now not any *choice* order of men, but *all* the sons of men are commanded to sing, as well as to pray, as has been shown above.

Objection 9: Where many sing together, as in a great mixed assembly, many sing what they do not know. And they that *do* know what they sing, cannot see, that many of the Psalms, which they sing, are not suitable to their own condition. And how then can they sing such Psalms, as songs of their own?

Answer 1: My first answer is that the ignorance of men in discerning the true matter, or the right manner of the duty, does not excuse them from performance of the duty. We speak of such moral duties, as the moral Law of God and the law of nature requires to be done. What if a man does not know what or how to pray? Yet that will not excuse him either from praying himself, or from joining with others that are better acquainted with prayer, than himself. So it is here, what if many men do not know what, or how to sing to God's Praise? Yet that will not excuse him, either from singing himself, or joining with others, that have more spiritual skill in that kind then himself.

Answer 2: My second answer is that it is an ignorance of a man's self, and of the ways of God to think that any Psalm is unsuitable to his own condition. For every Psalm sets forth both the attributes and works of God and his Christ, and this yields me a matter of holy reverence, blessing, and praise. Or else it describes the estate and ways of the Church and People of God, and this affects me with compassion, instruction, or imitation. Or else it deciphers the estate and ways of the wicked, and this holds forth to me a word of admonition. Or else it does lively express my own affections and afflictions, temptations and comforts, and then it furnishes men with fit matter and words to present their own condition before the Lord. But whatever the matter of the Psalm concerning God or his Christ, the godly, the wicked, myself, others, the good or evil estate of one, or any other, it never ministers fit matter and occasion to me of singing forth the praises of the Lord, since the name of God is to be blessed in all, whether it goes well or ill with ourselves or others.

CHAPTER 10:

Of the manner of singing.

The fourth and last head of scruples remains, touching on the manner of singing, concerning which a threefold scruple arises.

1. If it is lawful to sing Psalms devised by men.
2. If in tunes invented.
3. If it is lawful in order, before singing, to read the Psalm.

The two former of these scruples, because they stand on one and the same ground, may fitly be handled together.

The judgment of the Churches of Christ in these points, is *doubtless* suitable to their practice, "That it is lawful to sing Psalms in English verses, and in such grave and inglorious tunes, as well befits both the holiness and gravity of the matter, and the capacity of the singers."

A double reason may be given here. The first is this: If it is lawful to translate and turn the Hebrew bible into English prose in order to read, then it is lawful to translate David's Hebrew Psalms, and verse into our English Psalms and verse, in order to *sing*. But the former of these, is a confessed truth, and generally received among Protestants, except only Mr. Smith, who had a singular conceit in this point, "That all letters in the writings of the Old Testament were typical, and therefore would have all reading of the Holy Scripture to be abolished under the New Testament." But Christ himself commanded his disciples and the Pharisees to *search the Scriptures* in John 5:39. And how will they search them, except by reading them? And the noble and scholarly Bereans are commended for searching the Scriptures, in the examining of Paul's Doctrine (Acts 17:11-12). Which, how could they have done without reading? And therefore did all the Apostles and Evangelists write the New Testament in Greek? A language of all more generally known then the Latin, and therefore much more than any other in the world, as Tully himself rectifies (*Pro Archia Poeta*). Was it not for this end, that the New Testament might be read, and generally understood of all Nations? And where it was not understood, there it might most easily be translated out of a language well known to the several languages of every nation? And as for the Old Testament, it was translated to their hands out of the Hebrew into Greek almost three hundred years before the Apostles' times. Indeed, therefore God committed the whole counsel of his will and word to writing, for the edification and salvation of all his people, but that it might be read and understood of them all? If then it is the holy will of God, that the Hebrew Scriptures should be translated into English prose in order to read, then it is in like sort of his holy will, that the Hebrew

Chapter 10: Of the Manner of Singing?

Psalms, should be translated into English poems and verses in order for singing.

The consequence is *evident* and *undeniable*. For presupposing that God would have the Scriptures read of English men as well as other nations, then as a necessary means to that end, he would have the Scriptures translated into the English Tongue, that English People might be able to read them. In like sort, presupposing that God would have the Psalms of David, and other Scripture Psalms to be sung of English men then as necessary means to that end, he would have Scripture Psalms (which are poems and verses) to be translated into English Psalms (which are in like short poems and verses) that English people might be able to sing them. Now as all verses in all poems consist of a certain number and measure of syllables, so do our English verses (as they do in some other nations) run in meter also, which make the verses easier for memory, and fit for melody.

A second ground of this point is this. If it is not lawful to translate Hebrew Psalms into English, which run in number, measure, and meter of syllables, then it is not lawful to express the elegancy of the original language in a translation, for it is an artificial elegancy which the penmen of Scripture used that they penned the Psalms, and such like poetical books of Scriptures not in prose, but in verses, which observe a certain number and measure of syllables, and some of them run in meter also, as those know that know the Hebrew, and as Mr. Buxtorf shows in his *Thesaurus*, on page 629. Now, surely then it is a sacrilegious niceness, to think it is unlawfully lively to express all the artificial elegancies of the Hebrew text, so far as we are able to imitate the same in a translation. Indeed, doubtless it were a part of due faithfulness in a translator, as to declare the whole counsel of God, word for word, so to express lively every elegancy of the Holy Spirit, so that the people of God may be kindly affected, as well with the manner, as with the matter of the Holy Scriptures.

And for the English tunes that we use in singing Psalms, take this for a ground, since God has commanded us to sing psalms and hymns and spiritual songs, and among others, those of David. And yet with it has hid from us the Hebrew tunes, and the musical accents where the Psalms of David were accustomed to be sung. It must necessarily be that the Lord allows us to sing them in any such grave, and solemn and plain tunes, as do fitly suit the gravity of the matter, the solemnity of God's worship, and the capacity of a plain people. As to instance in a like case, when the Lord instituted the paschal Supper, and therein a whole Lamb to be eaten, the head sees and pertinences, and made no mention what drink they should use in it, whether wine, or water, beer, or other liquor. It was therefore left to their liberty, to use any such

Chapter 10: Of the Manner of Singing?

liquor as they were accustomed to drink fit for such meat as was to be eaten, and for such stomachs as were to feed on it. So here when the Lord appointed us to sing David's Psalms, and does not appoint us in what tunes, he therefore plainly leaves us to our liberty, to make use of such tunes as are suitable to such an ordinance, and to them that partake in it.

Objection 1: It will not follow that, because the word is to be dispensed in a known tongue, and so translated into it, therefore Hebrew Songs into English Songs. For the former, we have the warrant of the Word, to dispense it for edification, exhortation and comfort, but no word for the other, or no gifts of that kind given for the Church's profit, to dispense the word this way. Such songs therefore, and such tunes are not of God. Neither do I believe that the Levites invented any new tunes, I have no faith to believe that ever God trusted man's corrupt nature, to frame anything in God's worship to his praise. But suppose God had so far honored the worldly singers then, yet it will not follow, that the Lord Jesus allows us the like liberty now. He will not now allow any flesh to boast in his presence, who is not able to bring to pass so much as a good thought.

Answer 1: To weaken that argument for translating Hebrew songs into English songs and tunes, taken from the same warrant of translating Hebrew Scriptures into English Scriptures, this objection denies, that we have either the like word, or the like gift, or the like liberty. Where here our answer is, we have all alike equally.

For, 1. that we have the same word for singing Hebrew Songs, has been proved above, out of Colossians 3:16 and Ephesians 5:19. And the same word that commands us to sing them, commands us also the translation of Hebrew songs into English songs, as a necessary means to the acceptable singing of them. For if we should sing Hebrew songs in the Hebrew tongue, the People should sing without understanding, which were discretely contrary to the apostles' direction in 1 Corinthians 14:15.

Secondly, that we have also the like gift of translating Hebrew songs into the English songs, as well as Hebrew prose into English prose, is evident by the event. For we do not only have one, but many translations of the Hebrew Psalms into English Psalms, then of the Hebrew Bible into the English Bible.

Another Objection: "It is said that such a gift of translating Hebrew Songs into English Songs, is but a poetical gift, not a spiritual gift."

It might as well be said, that the translating of the Hebrew Scriptures into English, is not a spiritual gift, but a grammatical, or rhetorical gift. Whatever the art or skill may be, they are all gifts of God, and given chiefly for the service and edification of the Church of God.

Chapter 10: Of the Manner of Singing?

3. That we also have the same liberty of inventing tunes appears from what has been said already, for if God has given us liberty and warrant to sing psalms, hymns, and spiritual songs, then we must *sing* them in some *tunes*. Now the tunes of the temple are lost and hidden from us, so that we cannot sing them at all. And therefore we must sing other tunes, as are suitable to the matter, although invented by men.

You may ask, "But you do not believe that the Levites ever invented new tunes."

Either the Levites invented new tunes, or the Psalmists delivered musical accents, and notes together with the Psalms. Which seeing we do not understand, either we must not sing at all, or we must make use of such tunes as are invented by others.

You may say, but you cannot believe that God ever trusted man's corrupt nature to frame anything in God's worship to His Praise.

Then you cannot believe that God ever trusted the Hebrew and Greek Scriptures to be read in the Christian Churches in English words, for all English words are framed by English men, in corrupt nature, in other words, without the immediate assistance of the Holy Spirit in their framing. And if we may not make use of tunes invented by men for the singing of the Psalms, then neither may we make use of words invented by men for the *reading* of the Psalms, and other

Scriptures. The one is as much a worship of God as the other. And English words are as much as an invention of man as English tunes. But at least you should begin here to take up a scruple against the singing of Psalms in English tunes, and both on the pretense of the inventions of the men in the worship of God, do not be ignorant, that such godly men as have been desirous of reformation, and most zealous against human inventions in the worship of God, as had no warrant but the mind and will of man, not such as had warrant either from consequence of Scripture, or light of nature, or civil custom. For a woman to cover her head in the time of public prayer, or prophesying, and for a man to uncover his head, the Apostle warrants both from the light of Nature, and the custom of the Churches in 1 Corinthians 11:4-6.

The kiss of love in holy assemblies was warranted, not by divine institution, but by occasion of civil custom in those nations, where, it being usual in their civil assemblies to greet one another with a kiss of love. The Apostle does not disallow the use of it in holy assemblies, but only requires the sincerity and holiness of the love expressed in such kisses. (1 Corinthians 16:20, 1 Thessalonians 5:26, 1 Peter 5:14). The Apostles did not believe in this point as you do, that God never trusted corrupted nature, to frame anything in God's worship to his praise.

Chapter 10: Of the Manner of Singing?

It is true that a man's corrupt nature cannot bring forth a good thought, or a gracious thought, and that of itself, but yet by the help of Christ, it may bring forth both knowledge by tongues, and tunes by music, and that with as good allowance in the New Testament as in the Old. God did as much disallow any flesh to boast in his presence in the Old Testament, as in the New. But what cause has any flesh to boast, either of his spiritual or common gifts? Seeing that both are gifts, and received from God. And if received, why should men boast, as if they had not received them?

Objection 2: To sing with man's melody and meter, does not hold any spiritual gift of Christ, but only the art and nature of man. Whereas, prayer and preaching do hold forth spiritual gifts. And the tuning of Scripture by man's art, it is no gift of grace, neither does it redound to the praise of grace.

Although prayer and preaching hold forth spiritual gifts, yet all the duties that tend to edification, do not hold forth spiritual gifts, but some of them, common gifts only. The reading of the Scriptures tend to edification, as being itself an ordinance of God, although exposition afterwards is added as well, which is another ordinance in Deuteronomy 31:11-13. And yet reading of the Scriptures is no spiritual gift. Aquila, Symmachus, and Theodotian translated the Hebrew Scriptures into Greek, and yet none of them were endued with spiritual gifts, or at best but common. To say amen at the end of a public prayer, tends to edification, and yet *amen* may be said without holding any spiritual gift.

It is said, "But that which is the ground of your scruple seems to be that which is no gift of grace, how can it redound to the praise of Grace?"

But the answer is ready, that such things that help either the understanding, or the affection, and are appointed of God for his worship, they tend to edification, and so the praise of grace, though they may be performed by a gift of God in nature or art, without any spiritual gift of grace. Translation of the Scriptures into the mother tongue, and the reading of them in a known tongue, both of them help the understanding. And being appointed by God, they tend to the edification of the people in the grace of Christ. The translating of the Psalms into verse, in number, measure, meter, and suiting the ditty with apt tunes, helps to stir up the affections. And the singing of Psalms, being appointed of God, they tend to make a gracious melody to the praise of God and edification of his people. The ground of Aaron's Bells, and the blast of the silver trumpets, and the workmanship Hiram the Tyrian in Solomon's Temple, none of them held forth any spiritual gift of grace. The gift of God in nature and art might reach them all. Yet all of these, being appointed by God, putting forth these gifts, tended to the edification of the Church of God in the Grace of Christ.

Chapter 10: Of the Manner of Singing?

Objection 3: The meter of the late translators, although it comes nearer to the original, then the former meters, yet not so near as the prose. They frame their words and sentences more to the meter, then to the prose. Indeed, they sometimes break the attributes of God, and for the verse's sake put *Jah* instead of *Jehovah*, which is a mangling of the word.

Answer 1: The meter and verse of the latter translators, come as near to the words and sense of the original, as does the prose, especially considering that they did express it with the holy art of the original Hebrew poetry, which the prose does not attend to. Neither do the translators break the attributes of God, when for the verse's sake, they put *Jah* for *Jehovah*, for both *Jah* and *Jehovah* hold forth the same meaning and attributes of God, even his eternal being. The Evangelists and Apostles give us a pattern of greater changes of the attributes of God, then that, and yet without breaking the attributes of God, and much more without mangling the word of God. It is a usual thing with them to translate *Jehovah*, the Lord, in Matthew 22:44, with Psalm 110:1. And yet *Jehovah* holds forward his eternal essence, the term *Lord* his sovereign dominion. It was sacrilegious blasphemy to call this changing either the breaking of God's attributes, or the mangling of his word. Besides, it is very rare when the translators make any such change for Jah for Jehovah, and to prevent all stumbling, either of you, or others at it, I suppose that they will help it in the next edition of the Psalms.

Objection 4: What delight can the Lord take in such praises of himself, where sinful men or the man of sin has a hand in making the melody?

God delights that his will should be obeyed, at least he abhors that his will should be disobeyed, although by sinful men (1 Samuel 15:22-23). Since God commands all men in distress to call on him, and all men in their mirth, to sing His praise, what is mortal and sinful, that he should forbid, what God has commanded? God knows how to allow, and reward what is his own. When yet he takes no pleasure in the sinful manner of performance of any duty. God took notice of Ahab's humiliation, and rewarded it with respite of temporal judgments, although he took no pleasure in his sinful hypocrisy (1 Kings 21:27-29). And yet they that had a hand in making the melody of the English Psalms (whether in Old England or New), were men of a better spirit then Ahab. But I can but marvel, why you should put in the man of sin, as having any hand at all, in making this melody. For neither the man of sin, (by whom I supposed to mean Antichrist) or any Antichristian Church have had any hand in turning David's Psalms into English songs and tunes, or are accustomed to make any melody in the singing of them, yes, they reject them as *Geneva Jigs*, and they are cathedral priests of an

Chapter 10: Of the Manner of Singing?

Antichristian spirit, that have scoffed at Puritan Ministers, as calling the people to sing one of *Hopkins' Jigs*, and to hop up onto the pulpit. God keeps all Anti-Psalmists from the Antichristian Spirit. They that have been in an Antichristian Church can tell you, that Popish Churches are not accustomed to sing David's Psalms translated into verse in their own country meter, but they only sing the prose of David's Psalms in Cathedral notes. Which how far you yourselves are close to believing this, I leave to yourself to consider.

CHAPTER 11:

Of reading the Psalms in order before Singing.

The last scruple renaming in the manner of singing, concerns the order of singing after the reading of the Psalm. For it is doubted by some, and concluded by others, that reading of the psalms is not to be allowed in order to singing. We, for our parts easily grant, that where all have books and can read, or else can say the Psalm by heart, it is needless then to read each line of the Psalm beforehand, in order before singing. But if it is granted, which is already proven, that the Psalms are ordinarily sung in public, are *Scripture* Psalms, and they are those which are to be sung by the body of the congregation. Then to this end it will be a necessary help, that the words of the Psalm are openly read beforehand, line after line, or two lines together, that so they who lack either books or skill to read, may know what is to be sung and join with the rest in the duty of singing. It is not warrantable as an invention of man, brought into the worship of God, to make use of such means, which the light of nature teaches us, to be either necessary or convenient helps, either to the hearing or understanding of what is said in the worship of God. Scaffolds erected in meeting houses are inventions of men, by no express precept, or there is no example in Scripture calling for

Chapter 11: Of the Reading of Psalms before Singing?

them, and yet the light of nature easily suggests it, that they help to hear the word of God preached, an end to edification. They draw multitudes of people to sit within the minister's voice; that which helps the very outward sense of hearing, helps also knowledge and understanding, and so edification. And therefore, no man takes exceptions at scaffolds as inventions of men, although they are used to help forward God's worship, and spiritual edification, because they are not brought in, or used for spiritual means immediately, but remotely, so far as they are fit to help the outward sense of hearing, and understanding. Of the same use is reading in order to singing. It gives the people to hear, and so to understand, what is to be sung, so that they may join with the rest in singing of the Psalm. And by singing to be stirred up to use holy harmony, both with the Lord and his People.

Objection 1: The Scripture mentions no ordinary reading in any Church, but that which is joined with interpretation.

Answer 1: The Scriptures indeed mention Baruch to have read the word in a Church assembly, without adjoining any interpretation to it in Jeremiah 36:67.

Answer 2: As preaching of the word is an ordinance, so reading the word in order to preaching, is an ordinance as well. In like sort, as singing of Psalms is an ordinance, so reading the Psalms in order to singing, is allowable as well.

Answer 3: It is also mentioned in the Scripture, that the children of Israel did all join in singing the Song of Moses at the Red Sea in Exodus 15:1. Now it is not credible, that they who were bred and brought up in bondage were brought up to read. It was much if one of a thousand men could read. If most of them could not read, how could they join in singing the Psalms, unless some or other read, or pronounced the Psalm to them?

Answer 4: Although it is true that the Church of Israel had such an Ordinance amongst them, that after the reading of the Law, or the prophets, some or other of the priests or Levites, or prophets, were accustomed to expound the same to the people (Acts 13:15 and 15:21 and Nehemiah 8:7-8), yet the very reading of the word itself was also an ordinance, although no exposition followed. (Deuteronomy 31:11-13 and 27:14-26).

Objection 2: The Scripture prescribes now what Officer will perform this act, to read the Psalm in order to sing.

The Scripture prescribes this, as it also does with many other matters of ordering God's house, in other words, under general rules. It is nowhere expressly prescribed in Scripture who will be the mouth of the rest of the congregation in the public admonition, or excommunication of an offender, yet by general rules, it may easily be collected that public dispensations of the Church ordinarily pertain to

Chapter 11: Of the Reading of Psalms before Singing?

the public officers of the Church. Any of the preaching or ruling Elders may, with warrant, go before the people, in putting the words of the Psalm into their mouths.

Objection 3: This reading of the Psalm hinders the melody, the understanding, and the affection in singing.

If a man's prejudice against reading does not hinder himself, reading hinders none of these, not melody, for the reading is not in the art of singing, but in the pause, nor the understanding, for it helps such as cannot read, or lack of books to understand what is to be sung. Otherwise they could hardly perceive neither the affection, for then the melody is interrupted, the understanding furthered, and the affection is rather helped then hindered. Or if it is hindered, we should lay the fault where it is, rather in a coy or cold heart, then in a distinct and intelligent reading.

CHAPTER 12:

Answering the Objections brought from the ancient practice of the Primitive Churches.

Objection 1: The practice which was anciently used in the Churches immediately after the Apostles' times, is most probable to be nearest to the constitution of the Apostles, and that practice which followed a great while after it, is most probable to be the furthest away from their teachings. Now, the practice of singing Psalms which were made by the faithful, were first in use. For those Psalms which the Primitive Christians used before the day in the time of persecution, where they sang praises to Christ their God, (as Pliny writes to Trajan), they are said to be made of the faithful.

Answer 1: This Syllogism falls short of truth in both of the propositions. For it is not always true, that the practice which was used in the Churches immediately after the purest times, is nearest to their teachings (as the water is purest and clearest next to the fountain), and that which follows a great while after, is furthest away. As water near the fountain may call out to be troubled, and so become less clear and less pure, then in his running a course further off. The night following the day, although it might be nearer to the day, yet it is darker,

Chapter 12: The Ancient Practice of the Church

then the day following after, although it may be further off from the day before. The elders and people that lived in the days of Joshua, they served the Lord. But when that generation was gathered to their fathers, "There arose another generation after them, which knew not the Lord, and they did evil in the sight of the Lord, and served Balaam," (Judges 3:7-11). Paul forewarns the elders of Ephesus, he knew that after his departure, "grievous wolves should come in amongst them, not sparing the flocks," (Acts 20:29-30). And Eusebius complains out of Hesesippus, that after the Apostles' times, the Church did not remain a pure and undefiled virgin for long, (*History Eccles. Lib* 3, chapter 26).

Answer 2: Neither is true, that the practice of singing Scripture Psalms followed a great while after the Apostles' times, as if the faithful had only made use of their own personal gifts in compiling Psalms for the first three hundred years. For it is evident that in the next century after the Apostles' times, the Church either practiced out of the Holy Scriptures, or out of their own gift. Yes, and Pliny himself, which is all the testimony you allege of the Churches practice for three hundred years, does not express what Psalms they sang, or whether out of the Holy Scriptures or not, or that anyone sang solely for the congregation. But that they did meet before day to sing praises to God and Christ, and to administer discipline.

Answer 3: Although they had made use of their personal gifts, more than they did in the times of the primitive persecutions, during the first three hundred years, yet that would not argue that they neglected the use of David's Psalms, much less would it encourage us to neglect the use of David's psalms now. During the times of those bloody persecutions, as the sufferings of the Saints abounded, so did their consolations through Christ abound as well. As God honored sundry of them with miraculous gifts, so especially with a large measure of spiritual joy in the Lord, which might furnish them with more enlargement of heart, to compile Psalms to set forth his praise, then God is accustomed to bestow in more peaceable times.

Answer 4: Although they sometimes sang Scripture Psalms, and sometimes spiritual songs by personal gifts. Both sorts evidence the judgment and practice of those times, touching vocal singing. They did not only make melody to the Lord with Grace in their hearts, but with Songs also in their mouths. Justin the Martyr (who flourished within fifty years after the Apostles' time), or whoever was the author of those questions and answers among his works, although he speaks of musical instruments, as utterly unfit for Church Assemblies, yet, "simple singing with the voice he much magnifieth, as that which stirreth up the heart to spiritual joy, and holy desires, as that which subdueth the passions and concupiscence of the flesh, as that which scatters the evil suggestions of spiritual enemies, as that which waters, and refreshes the soul to fruitfulness in good duties, as that which stirs up courage and constancy in wrestling for the truth, and as that which giveth some medicine to all the grief, which befall a man through sad and sorrowful accidents in this life," (*Ans. to Ques.* 107, *ad Orthodox.*).

Answer 5: After the three hundred years after Christ left the earth, and not long after the times of persecution returned in the days of Julian the Apostate, when the Children of Antioch, together with the women and children, sang such Psalms of David as cursed and reproached heathen idols and idolaters, (*Socrates Eccles. History* lib. 2. Chapter 16 in *Gn.* Chapter 18. Theodoret expresses by name Psalm 115 and 68 in *History Eccles.* lib 3. Chapter 17.).

Finally, although before the three hundred years were expired, we read in Eusebius, that one Nepos (though a millinery), was well respected, as for other good gifts and works, so for diverse psalms and hymns composed by him (which some brethren did willingly use a long time after), yet we suppose, that was such a practice as yourself would not allow, to sing set forms of Psalms invented by men, and to continue to sing them after their departure, and in the meantime, to refuse set forms of Psalms, indicted by the Holy

Spirit, as if the Psalms indicted by an extraordinary measure of the Spirit, were more unclean, then the Psalms indicted by the common gift of an ordinary elder or brother.

Objection 2: Samosatenus the Heretic (who denied the deity of the Lord Jesus),was the first that within those first three hundred years, opposed this by singing personal gifts.

Answer 1: Not out of respect to David's Psalms, but to avoid the hymns which set forward the glory and Godhead of Christ, and to bring in Psalms, which did set forth his own heresy, along with his own praises, as Eusebius testifies.

Objection 3: The practice of singing David's Psalms was a later invention, brought into the Church of Antioch by Flavianus and Diodorus. And so this custom was taken up by Ambrose and Augustine, but vehemently opposed by Hilary, a ruler there, because they sang out of a book. So Augustine turned a patron for it, and forced it there rather by the importunity of the people, then of his own accord. As being destitute of weapons out of the word of God for it, and therefore afterwards repented for it, and had the customs removed.

Answer 1: My first answer is that Tertullian's testimony alleged above, evidently evinces that the singing of Scripture Psalms was in use in the Church before Flavianus and Theodorus were born, (*Apologet.* cap. 39).

Answer 2: My second answer is that, the practice brought in by Flavianus and Diodorus, was rather some new fashion of singing Psalms, then the singing of them. For as Theodoret reports it, they were the first that divided the choir of singers into two sides, and appointed one side of them to answer the other in the singing of them, and used the same at the monuments of the dead, and that sometimes all night long. But these inventions favored rather of superstition, then of pure primitive devotion. Although they wrought a good effect on Theodosius, Flavianus sent those songs to be sung at his table, to moderate his wrath against the citizens of Antioch, (Theodoret, *Hist. Eccles. lib.* 2 Chapter 24. Zozomen, *Hist. Eccles.* lib. 7. Chap. 23).

Answer 3: My third answer is that it is spoken without warrant of antiquity that Ambrose and Augustine took up the practice of singing David's Psalms from Flavianus and Diodorus. For neither did they bring it in, and neither was it the slackness of some Churches receiving an ordinance, a just exception against the ordinance, but rather a just reprehension of their negligence. And so much does Augustine confess in his 199th *Epistle*, page 18. "Where speaking of this practice of singing Psalms, though it be so useful to the stirring up of the heart in godliness, and to kindle the affection of divine reading. Yet the custom of Churches is diverse about it, and the most members of the African Churches, *Pigrioria sunt*, have been more slothful in receiving it. Insomuch that the natives reprehend us, that we sing soberly the divine songs of the Prophets, whereas they inflame their drunkenness by a trumpet of exhortation to the singing of Psalms, composed by their own human wit."

By which reproof of the natives, it may appear that the custom of singing David's Psalms was in use in the African Churches, and in Millain also of former times, and that the custom that was brought into the Church of Millain to keep the people awake in their night watches against the Arian violence, was the singing of Psalms after the Eastern manner, with more curiosity of music, and one side of the singers answering another. And of this is Augustine to be understood in the ninth book of his *Confessions*, chapter 7.

Answer 4: My fourth answer is that, it is not true that Augustine became a patron of singing David's Psalms, rather forced to it by the importunity of the people then of his own accord. For he says in the same chapter of the same epistle, that "The practice of singing Psalms and Hymns is to be done without doubting, seeing it may be defended out of the Scriptures, in which we find both the Doctrines, and Examples, and precepts of Christ, and of his Apostles for it." And the same Augustine, in his first tome and third rule,

Chapter 12: The Ancient Practice of the Church

writes, "Do not simply sing, but what you *read* is to be sung, but that which is *not* written that it should be sung, do not sing it. Neither is it true that Augustine repented, that the custom of singing David's Psalms was brought into the Church, or that he wished that it were taken away instead."

Although, when he saw his heart taken up more with the melody of the tune, then with the sweetness of the matter, he could have wished the sweetness of the melody removed from his own ears, and from the Church, yet still he would have them sung after the manner of the Church of Alexandria, and Athanasius. And then, correcting himself, he says, "But when I remember my tears which I poured out at the singing of thy Church, in the first restoring of my faith, and how I am still moved, not with the Song, but with the matter sung, when it is sung with a clear voice, and convenient tune or modulation, I do again acknowledge the great utility of this institution."

And although he wavers between the peril of delight to the sense, and experiment of wholesomeness to the soul, his scruple was not of the lawfulness of singing David's Psalm, but partly of the pleasantness of the tunes (which might be more artificial then the gravity of the ordinance required) partly of the expediency to himself, until his heart was more spiritual. His writing against *"Hillarius jubentibus fratriibus,"* does not argue, he wrote against his will, but by a good call, in defense of singing David's Psalms against a man that took up any occasion to carp at God's Ministers (Augustine, *Retract.* Lib 2. Chapter 11).

Objection 4: It is to be noted that forms of divine service and litanies begun to be used at the same time, in many places. In the French Churches, and in Constantine's court and camp, both himself and his soldiers, using a form of prayer, the Churches grew proud and lazy. At which time they also had their regular and canonical singers appointed there by office. The Psalms being composed by private Christians (whom they call idiots), being interdicted in one and the same counsel of Laodicea, until eventually it was turned into a pageant in the year 666, the fatal figure of the Antichrist. It being impossible that the lively gifts of God's Spirit in his people should breathe any longer when forms are once set up in the Church.

Answer 1: Although Constantine appointed a form of prayer to his soldiers, we do not read that he limited them to the use of it, much less that forms of divine service and litanies were brought into the Church in his time, or even a hundred years later. And regular and canonical singers were *not* brought into the Church in his time. The Council of Laodicea

Chapter 12: The Ancient Practice of the Church

which allowed them, and interdicted Psalms composed by private Christians, was about sixty years after him.

Answer 2: Their forbidding anybody to sing, except for those who were appointed to sing, though they did it to abuse the people's abuse of the Psalms by singing out of tune, yet their care might better have been bestowed in teaching the people to know and keep the tune, and in advising such as had low and strong voices, and were skilled with music, to have led and kept the people in a decent melody. But otherwise, for their prohibiting of singing Psalms composed by private men, and the reading of any books in the Church except for the Bible, so that they might establish the reading of Scripture books, and the singing of Scripture Psalms. It is so far from superstition, that it tends rather to prefer divine institutions above human inventions. When they interdicted the Psalms composed by private Christians, who they called idiots. You are not ignorant that an idol in their language does not signify anything by a private man, and in the same sense the Apostle himself uses it, although the translators make it to mean the unlearned, (1 Corinthians 14:16).

Neither do forms of God's Praise stop the breathing of the lively gifts of God's Spirit, when the forms are no other but as were indicted by the immediate inspiration of the Holy Spirit, for when the Psalms were commended to the Church of Israel, and by them were ordinarily sung in the Temple and elsewhere, would you say it hindered the free passage of breathing? Or the lively gifts of God's Spirit? Either in the ministry of the Priests, or in the writings and sermons of the Prophets? Surely Elisha found it different in 2 Kings 3:15, and the whole Church of Judah. As for 666 (which you call the fatal figure of the Antichrist), judge you in your own soul before the Lord does, whether it does more favor of an Antichristian spirit, for the whole Church to sing the Psalms of David with one accord, or to sing *Te Deum*, or some other anthem devised by a private spirit, one man alone? Surely it is. Antichristian Churches utterly reject the singing of David's Psalms in the meter of each nation in their mother tongue, and also reproach such Psalms as Geneva lies. They are so far off from closing with their singing as an invention of their own.

Objection 5: Let no man think that the singing of Psalms is an ordinance of God, because many Christians have found their affections stirred (as Augustine did) in the singing of them. This does not justify this practice any more then it does preaching by a false calling, because some have found conversion by it. It does not justify it any more than receiving the seal of the supper in a false Church, and that with the Idolatrous gesture of kneeling, because some have found quickening and strengthening grace there. For God's goodness many times goes beyond his truth.

Answer 1: We cannot say that God's goodness goes beyond his truth, although sometimes he shows a man mercy out of his way. For we have the truth of God's word to testify, that sometimes he converts men like Saul on his way to Damascus. But we say that when God does this, he either convinces a man the error of his way before showing him favor in it, or else the way itself or duty is of God, although there is some failing in the circumstance of it. Much of Israel that came to the Passover in Hezekiah's time in their uncleanliness, found mercy with the Lord. But it was because of the ordinance and duty was of God, the failing was only in the manner of preparation of it (2 Chronicles 30:18-20). But if Micah set up an invention of his own in his house, although he may promise himself a blessing in some orderly circumstance of it, (as he did in Judges 17:13), let him be sure that he will find a curse instead of a blessing, according as God had expressed it in Deuteronomy 7:26. It is granted and bewailed, that there has been found some sinful failings in sundry circumstances of some ministers' callings. And yet because the substance of the calling was of God, many have found saving blessings in attending on their ministry. And the Lord's Supper administrated by them being of God, although it was the gesture in which it was received that was corrupt; the Lord was pleased to accept and bless what was his own, and to pass by sins of ignorance in his people. But can it ever be proved that when any practice of God's worship has been nevertheless blessed with the communication of spiritual affections, and that not seldom and rarely, but frequently and usually, not to one or two saints, but generally, not to the weakest, but to the strongest Christians? We are very persuaded that no such instance can be given since the world began. God is not accustomed to honor and bless superstitions with the reward of sincere devotion. But surely, God has delighted to bless the singing of his Holy Psalms, with gracious and spiritual affections, but only in Augustine's time, and in Justin Martyr before him. But from age to age he also blesses his saints, usually, generally, and abundantly, so that doubtless the servants of God defraud their souls of much spiritual good, and comfort, who defraud themselves of the fellowship of this *ordinance*.

But here is the misery of the present age, that those ordinances that men have practiced, either without the knowledge of the true grounds there, or without the life and sense of the comfort of them, or without the sincere love of them, they have therefore afterwards in the hour and power of temptation cast them aside, and so forsaken the holy institutions of God, to embrace and please themselves in their *own imaginations*. How much safer is it for sincere Christians to walk in God's Holy fear, and in the sense of their own ignorance, infirmities, and temptations, to suspect their own private apprehensions? And how much safe is it to humbly beg the Spirit of Life and Truth, to lead them into all truth, and meekly consult with their brothers without setting up any idol or forestalled imagination in their hearts, before they resolve to run in a different way, to the grief and scandal of their kin? It is a palsy distemper in a member to be carried with a different motion from the rest of the body.

May the Lord heal our swerving, and stabilize us with a Spirit of *truth* and *grace* in Jesus Christ.

FINIS

www.ingramcontent.com/pod-product-compliance
Lightning Source LLC
Chambersburg PA
CBHW032004080426
42735CB00007B/503